Handwriting Analysis at Wor[...]

FRITS COHEN is an Anglo-Dutch [...] who in the 1970s became interested in graphology through his experience in human resource management. He is an expert document examiner, analysing, for example, signatures on cheques, comparing documents and providing testimony on the authenticity of handwriting samples. He has been using graphology for years in the selection of personnel for commerce, especially sales, and in manufacturing and other fields. Five years ago, he decided to use his own team of professional graphologists, trained on the continent of Europe, to establish handwriting analysis in the UK. In partnership with Daniel Wander he founded Graph-O-Logica Ltd to provide this service to UK and overseas companies.

DANIEL WANDER is a psychologist and a barrister. His interest in human resource management developed during his role as legal adviser and consultant to the UK Citizens' Advice Bureau, and during his business experience as MD of several companies. He later became a JP. After qualifying in psychology, he focused on counselling and later set up Graph-O-Logica with Frits Cohen.

The drawings are the result of an intensive, whirlwind, artistic co-operation between Mrs Liuba Kostenko, a gifted Russian painter and illustrator from St Petersburg, and Frits Cohen, who paints for pleasure.

The two met at the National Gallery, London; an invitation to Frits' studio ensued and, in spite of linguistic difficulties, he expressed the ideas, mainly in gestures, whilst Liuba reacted with her uniquely creative drawings.

Liuba has exhibited extensively in the former Soviet Union since 1973, as well as in Belgrade, Bulgaria, Austria, Finland, Sweden and Germany.

Handwriting Analysis at Work

Fritz Cohen
and Daniel Wander

Thorsons
An Imprint of HarperCollins*Publishers*

Thorsons
An Imprint of HarperCollins*Publishers*
77–85 Fulham Palace Road,
Hammersmith, London W6 8JB
1160 Battery Street
San Francisco, California 94111–1213

Published by Thorsons 1993
10 9 8 7 6 5 4 3 2 1

The signatures illustrated on the front cover
have been taken from publicly available sources.
They are unrelated to the contents of this book.

A catalogue record for this book
is available from the British Library

ISBN 0 7225 2637 7

Phototypeset by Harper Phototypesetters Limited,
Northampton, England
Printed in Great Britain by
Mackays, Chatham, Kent

Contents

Introduction

Every individual is a kaleidoscopic masterpiece of infinitely varying behaviour and thought patterns, traits and qualities. To really understand people, you have to see and analyse every facet of their personality. It isn't enough to observe their behaviour — you need to comprehend their subjective motivation, to see reality as they experience it. You must understand how they adapt to the outside world: how they handle human relationships; how they react to hurt and aggression. You have to know how they mould and change circumstances to suit themselves.

What you see on the outside is a compromise between an individual's needs and the demands of reality. To penetrate the façade, to understand the whole person, takes training, a knowledge of psychology and careful observation. Acquiring these skills takes dedication and, above all, time.

People whose work involves recruiting staff and managing people need fast, accurate insight into character. To get the best out of the individuals and teams they lead, managers have to know the abilities and shortcomings of all their staff, and to assess rapidly how a newcomer would react with the team, get on with the boss and fit into the company culture. An in-depth profile of everyone in their workforce would be a time-saving short cut. But what they really need is a dependable picture, right back at recruitment stage, of each candidate's personality from the standpoint of suitability for the job.

To build up such a picture you need a lot of detailed information. You must have an accurate profile of each candidate's personality and character. You also need to know in advance how they will react to pressures or action imposed on them in specific work situations. Methods usually used to obtain such information range from interviewing techniques to complex testing procedures.

Interviewing assessed

Most managers and bosses pride themselves on their ability to pick out a winner. Interviewing is the favourite method of assessing candidates for selection, a method used by 99 per cent of people in the business of recruiting staff. Yet many professionals deprecate the efficiency of interviewing. Perhaps this is because they feel that there is often a big discrepancy between the first impression of someone at interview and how that person works out in the job.

Why does this happen? Because although people say they are objective at interview, in practice they find it difficult to exclude their subjective convictions and preferences. It is easy for the less experienced interviewer to be deceived by appearances and taken in by charm, verbal fluency or downright deception. When interviewing, you might be unconsciously prejudiced for or against a person's sex, shape, skin colour or ethnic group. And you could be put off by, say, an assertive or reserved manner — or even something as irrelevant as the size of a candidate's nose.

Because of the perceived inadequacy of interviewing, many professionals have introduced practical performance tests to back them up. Tests for skills — speed and accuracy for keyboard operators, or familiarity with specific computer

The interview reversed

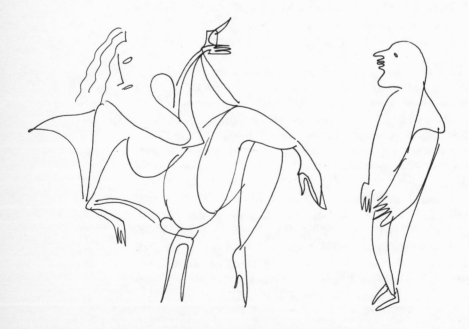

packages; the ability to do a typical task for a technician — are obviously useful for assessing knowledge and practical abilities, but they tell you little about an applicant's personality.

Following the same line of thought, many companies use psychometric tests. Psychometrics is the part of psychology concerned with psychological testing and the statistical methods involved in assessing the results of such tests. Psychometric testing is especially popular in the UK, where it was pioneered by the discredited Cyril Burt, who trained the influential psychometric psychologists R.B. Cattell and Hans Eysenck. There are more than 5,000 different psychometric tests, designed to measure intelligence, numeracy, motivation, aptitude and other personal characteristics. Tests for personnel selection are often designed to assess personality. Such tests take different forms, but many are based on multiple-choice questions: 'Tick the answer that most closely describes you: a) I always like to win; b) I get on well with most people' and the like.

The results are measured in terms of a correlation coefficient (the degree to which two variables correspond) and personality tests tend to correlate at around 0.3 ~~per cent~~ with various job performance measures.

There are many reasons for such poor results:

- Many such tests are poorly designed — for example, tests intended to measure intelligence are applied to personality-testing — and many are designed as a compromise between high profitability, tester-convenience and sales potential, followed by an assumed quality of results.
- The tests are often wrongly used. For instance, employers may make erroneous assumptions about what qualities are needed by a salesperson, say, or an administrator.
- Predictive tests, designed to reveal the future success of a particular individual in a specific position or situation, are especially unreliable. They tend to overstate successful candidates' competence, simply because the knowledge required to make such predictions is incomplete. Predictive tests do not take into consideration such crucial factors as whether colleagues are going to be accommodating or hostile, or the boss subject to moods, and how candidates will react in these situations. Individual performance depends partly on outside factors, such as company culture, and a person's reaction to it.

- Psychometric tests are often marked by people who don't have the statistical skills to assess such complex data.

The end result of these flaws is, in a word, failure. Tests must be reliable to be valid, and it is clear from the results that these apparently objective psychological tests do not measure what they are supposed to. Practice has shown that the validity and usefulness of all psychometric tests and techniques is at best questionable, at worst non-existent or low. They can be taught and faked; practice makes perfect. Professor Paul Kline, the UK's only professor of psychometrics, stresses that the results need skilful amplification through other methods and that testing 'is rendered inane and defeated in case of subtle topics for reason of the crude and inferential nature of even the best psychometric tests' (*Psychology Exposed*, p.63).

Nevertheless, many companies in the UK claim to make use of personality tests in their selection or assessment procedures. Some large companies arrange for prospective executives to undergo a battery of such tests, at assessment centres. These take a number of days, with several assessors observing each candidate's behaviour in practical and simulated work situations. The cost of such intensive testing is such that only candidates for the most elevated or most crucial jobs are subjected to this technique. If the wrong person is then chosen, the cost rises to astronomical heights.

Should we take the chance?

Employing people is expensive. The real cost of one employee is 70 per cent to 200 per cent above basic salary, when you take into consideration equipment and accommodation costs. Employ the wrong person and this figure escalates to include hidden costs: dissatisfied employers and disaffected staff, a high turnover in personnel, increased absenteeism through illness, wasted training, inefficiency, team breakdown, unmet targets, loss of sales and clients. Management needs to get a grip on the situation. To do so involves making the unpredictable more manageable.

Handwriting: the key to character

Handwriting analysis, also called graphology, deals with the assessment of character from handwriting. As a method of appraising personality, and the suitability of people for work and other situations, it is objective, fast and accurate. As long as the writing is expertly analysed, and interpreted with a specific job situation in mind, graphology is more reliable than any other character-assessment technique on the market.

In France, the Netherlands and several other EC countries, in Switzerland and in the USA, handwriting analysis is a standard tool in the selection of personnel for key jobs — executives, representatives, supervisors, personnel assistants, sales and marketing executives, and managers.

Interest in handwriting analysis has been growing in the UK as a result of increased trade with other EC countries. For example, several UK branches of French companies expect staffing agencies to put forward suitable candidates on the basis of commissioned handwriting analysis, as well as their c.v. and past experience.

And handwriting analysis is, in itself, interesting. What is more fascinating than studying yourself and learning to understand other people better? It is an absorbing subject to study for pleasure.

More important at the moment, however, may be the need to know about how useful handwriting analysis can be in your business. Although many of the most successful international companies use it to their advantage — Warburgs is an outstanding example — very little information is available about occupational graphology. There is an urgent need for clarity and information. This book seeks to provide them.

Learning to write

Handwriting analysis is based on the knowledge that your handwriting is as unique as your fingerprints. You learned to write years ago at school by copying the letters of the alphabet onto ruled paper from a copybook or a blackboard. Later, you learned to join the letters up. Although, at first, you strove to copy the letters exactly, as you developed expertise in this new skill you modified your writing. You may have slanted your letters leftward or rightward, or begun to write into the margins, or closer to the line above. Perhaps you made some letters smaller or bigger; perhaps you closed up the spaces between the words — or widened them.

What caused you to make these subtle changes were certain fundamental traits of character — a depressed or pessimistic person might tend to write downward-sloping lines; a careless person might forget to dot every 'i'. Since the mid-seventeenth century, when Camillo Baldi first studied the connection between character and handwriting (*see* p.28), interested people have studied handwriting, and made more and more connections. It is now established that an individual's style of writing is mainly influenced not by the conscious will, but by the unconscious mind. Handwriting should really be called 'brainwriting', as Professor Wilhelm Preyer wrote in 1895 (*see* p.28).

Copybook styles: examples used for teaching.

USA, *c.1870, designed by Thomas E. Hill. This style was very influential.*

ABCDEFGHIJKLMNOPQRSTUVWXYZ

abcdefghijklmnopqrstuvwxyz

USA, c.1980. Palmer script.

ABCDEFGHIJKLMNOPQRSßTUVWXYZ

abcdefghijklmnoprstuvwxyz

Germany, c.1980.

ABCDEFGHIJKLMNOPQRSTU
WVXYZ abcdefghijklmnopqrst
uvwxyz

Holland, c.1980.

ABCDEFGHIJKLMNOPQRSTU
VWXYZ
abcdefghijklmnopqrstuvwxyz

British, contemporary. Trend towards simplification; does it fulfil
the need for legibility and speed, together with user-friendliness
and future computer acceptability?

Scientific handwriting analysis, then, is based on observation and measurement, and the objective evaluation of the results. The analyst is trained to notice, for example, the distances between words, variations in the formation of letters, movement, ways of connecting letters, slant and pressure. The apportioning of significance to each handwriting characteristic and assessing its part in the overall picture is a skill that is built up over time and as a result of experience. The value of this skill has been proven in practice.

The key to successful recruitment

There are two types of handwriting analyst. Most people have heard of handwriting experts, who examine the physical structure of writing. Theirs is a technical appraisal. They are often asked to testify in court whether two handwriting samples have been written by the same person or whether one is a forgery.

The graphologist, on the other hand, deals with character, assessing the significance of the structural elements that make up a person's script and using them to peel off conscious and unconscious layers of the mind to draw a stunningly accurate portrait of the writer. Graphologists portray people in writing, without ever having seen them. Their reports are used by managing directors, personnel managers and human resource managers to complement interviews and pinpoint help with annual assessment of staff. Graphology is also used by professionals in selection agencies and marriage bureaux for compatibility assessment.

Some of these professionals work by asking certain clients — and candidates for the more important jobs — for handwriting samples. They send them, together with background information, such as a job description, to professional handwriting analysts for graphological test reports. These tests have the advantage of being specific to the client's needs, and — unlike psychological tests — as fake-proof as fingerprints. They are holistic, recording unconscious desires and motivations, as well as aptitude and ability; and examining feelings and emotions without the tension and embarrassment that are present at interview.

Executives who have departed from other, standard assessment methods have had remarkably increased success rates in finding the right person for the job, plus far better personnel retention rates, at a fraction of the cost of psychological testing. The many clients returning year after year for graphological tests carried out by the company run by the authors of this book do so because they have witnessed the validity of the results. Coupled with well worked-out job descriptions and structured interviews (*see* Chapter 2), handwriting analysis by experienced analysts is the most reliable method of candidate selection.

Learning to interpret handwriting

Ideally, perhaps, experts' reports should be the standard first stage in the selection of candidates for every job. Obviously, practical considerations of time, cost and convenience make it impossible for any organization to send every applicant's handwriting to an outside expert before a selection is made. The obvious way forward is not an escape from responsibility into a battery of dubious psychometric tests, but for the concerned manager and personnel officer to acquire insight into the skills of the handwriting analyst.

In France this has already happened. There, senior management tends to be more directly involved in selection and recruitment procedures for the most crucial positions than in the UK. In many EC countries wages and added taxes for social security are considerably higher than in the UK, and the cost of dismissing someone is very high. For these reasons, executives like to keep firm control over the quality of their human resources and of the newcomers selected to join their teams.

Few managers, directors of selection bureaux and agencies, or human resource managers, will want to become professional graphologists. But careful study of this book will certainly help you produce better-defined job profiles, improve your interviewing techniques and give you a clearer view of how to assess a candidate's suitability for a specific job. You will also save on re-advertising, re-interviewing and retraining for staff replacements. You will gain a deeper understanding of the people you work with and be able to improve teamwork among them.

How does it work? Do you need scientific training? Like psychology, graphology is an amalgam of study, research, experience and capability. It is a diagnostic science. It requires dedication. And to penetrate the superficial image, to discover an individual's driving force, you need hawk-like observation, combined with perception.

Analysing handwriting involves two main processes. When you analyse — observe and dissect — a sample, your brain follows and notes the logical sequences of the facts you write down. Your thinking, summarized in your notes, polarizes and categorizes the writing in the sample in front of you.

Written language is the manipulation of symbols within a framework of rules, such as grammar, mathematics and logic. The software with which your brain is programmed is based on critical thinking, i.e. you decide in favour of or against a certain interpretation, on the revealing of the truth through logic, argument, measurement and other scientific methods. This processing logic is a pre-programmed passive information system.

As Edward de Bono explains in his book *I am right, you are wrong*, there are different types of logic: rock logic and water logic. Rock logic is based on accepted hard facts, thus without the element of perception. Like a computer data-base, it has to be manipulated by outside input to obtain answers: correct or incorrect, positive or negative. It is fortunate that our brain with its neural network does not work just like a present-day computer — it would take us days just to get dressed. Imagine that you had to work out how to hold a toothbrush each time you brushed your teeth, how to squeeze toothpaste on to it, how to brush with it. And the sequence of each action!

Luckily the brain behaves as a self-organizing pattern system, not static, but able to adjust itself to circumstances like water adjusts its form to differently shaped containers. It is therefore able to set up routines for everyday use. The *The graphologist* patterns formed by its network of nerves are not *as detective* symmetrical. They shift, jumping away from the obvious

path on to side tracks, suddenly opening up new perspectives on the way.

This process produces humour, creativity and poetry. It is a form of perception caused by 'lateral thinking' (as De Bono terms it). We are taught logic, but we are not taught perception.

Merely analysing data will not produce the ideas necessary to construct a cohesive written portrait of a person from his or her handwriting. That needs perception, insight and creative design, in the sense of putting things together. It is a process of scanning, jumping, side-tracking and suddenly becoming aware of new aspects.

Handwriting analysis, then, is creative design in its widest context, not just in its usual sense of visual appearance. It involves conceptual effort as well as constructive and creative thinking.

As you can see, handwriting analysis is a complex subject. A little knowledge is a dangerous thing, so don't expect to be able to use the knowledge you acquire from reading this book without practice. Be prepared to make many 'dummy runs' before you can really trust your judgement.

Finally, you must always respect your subjects' confidentiality. Graphologists who belong to the International Association for Business Graphology observe a professional ethical code that requires them to respect privacy and avoid intrusion into the strictly private areas of personality that are of no professional concern. You must adhere strictly to the same principles.

What handwriting analysis will not reveal

The writer's age: Mental and physical age may differ substantially.

The writer's sex: We all have traces of the opposite sex in us. The writing will indicate predominant traits which may have male or female connotations.

The writer's future: Circumstance, surroundings and culture are factors beyond the analyst's observations. The graphologist can, however, express an opinion based on the character, traits and capacities detected in the script and relate them to the known requirements of a job.

The writer's outward appearance: Eyes, hair and skin colour cannot be revealed by the writing.

Using this book

Very little information is available about using graphology in business. This book fills that vacuum. It is written for professional people who want to obtain primary know-how: directors, managers, educators, students of psychology and related subjects, doctors, psychotherapists, personnel officers, headhunters and heads of selection agencies.

Before you start, you need to collect a set of handwriting samples to analyse. Select three or four people you know well, of different character. Note their sex and age. If you can, ask them to write on A4 unlined paper with a ballpoint or a fountain pen. Their writing should be spontaneous, relaxed and original — so no copies of poems or anything written by other people. A sample of 15 to 20 lines or more, with a salutation and a signature, is all you need. The same samples can be used over and over again to work through the various aspects of their analysis, as detailed in the analytical chapters further ahead:

- **Chapter 1** explains how graphology developed, explores the connection between graphology and psychology, and sets handwriting analysis in its present and future context.
- **Chapter 2** looks at the importance of a carefully written advertisement and a detailed job specification in producing an accurate analysis. It advises on the layout of an application form, and how to ask for a handwriting sample; and explains backup procedures in the selection process, such as interview check lists. It also discusses the use of graphology in yearly assessment tests for progress, success or failure, a rise or promotion.
- **Chapters 3 and 4** — the main body of the book — detail how to interpret handwriting, and how to assess positive and negative personality features.
- **The Appendices** at the back of the book contain samples of handwriting — some by famous living people — and examples of their interpretation and analysis. There is also a list of useful addresses and other books to read.

Feedback

This is the first book to explain how to apply handwriting analysis to business, the professions and to work in general, and we are confident that your reading time will be amply rewarded. We invite positive criticism, suggestions for improvement and additions for future print-runs. Readers are further invited to contribute details of results by interview plus handwriting analysis, monitored over a period of time, to our records. Please write to us at: Graph-O-Logica Ltd, 48 Oakleigh Park South, London N20 9JN.

1 What is Graphology?

Your handwriting is uniquely yours, as accurate a symbol of your identity as your gene structure. No two people — even identical twins — will produce identical writing. The law accepts this by recognizing the validity of agreements that have been signed. You recognize it by signing a cheque and expecting the bank to accept it as yours.

As long as people have written with pen and ink, they have wondered why people write differently. And they have supposed that the character of the writer must determine writing style. In the second century AD the Roman historian Suetonius Tranquillus observed in his book *De Vitae Caesarum* (Life of Caesar) that the handwriting of the Emperor Octavius Augustus clearly showed his economy. Augustus spaced his words very closely together, and wherever possible added a few letters at the ends of the lines.

Copybook style

Primary school teachers, in a unique position to observe and compare the development of children's writing from the first stages, see the rapid emergence of an easily recognizable personal handwriting style. This is despite the fact that all the children will have begun by copying the same standard example (called 'copybook' style, *see* pp.14—15).

It is the differences that develop from the copybook style that make each person's handwriting unique. As people mature, their handwriting changes. And, the reasoning goes, if the differences are caused by character traits, then handwriting must be a key to the writer's personality. To put it simplistically, by closely observing many people and their handwriting, and by linking personality traits to writing style, a general guide to character analysis can be produced.

Copybook: the way children learn to write from the school model. Basic signs, movements, examples of letters and connections.

Exercises for script.

Examples of exercises for cursive writing.

In order to begin the analysis the graphologist needs to have knowledge about the way the writer was taught to write. Each country has its own copybook styles. Its Embassy may provide examples, or the British Library may hold some. It is the divergence from copybook which distinguishes and characterizes each individual. Even children show this individuality: their teacher recognizes them immediately by their script.

Our classroom rules

① Dont talk when the teacher is talking.
② Keep your drawer tidy.
③ Dont write on the tables.
④ Dont damage other peoples belongings .
⑤ Keep your books in good condition .
⑥ Ask before you take something that does'nt belong to you.

The black smooth material melted and was dripping with something. It only smelt a bit but when it had burnt it was curled up and smelt. When the fabric was held near it just curled up and the flame took 15 seconds to die down

The Queen was walking through Westminster Abbey and I lived in the nearest town to Westminster. In our family it was just me and my mother. My father had been murdered about 10 years ago and I could only remember him from the pictures I saw. Anyway

London, 1992. Eleven-year-old pupils; lined paper with margins.

Terror of the Sea

It was the sea that Mafatu feared. He had been surrounded by it ever since he was born. The thunder of it filled his ears; the crash of it upon the reef, the mutter of it at sunset, the threat and fury of its storms. on every hands wherever he turned - the sea.

Terror of the Sea

It was the Sea that Maftu feared. He had been had been surrounded by it ever since he was born. The thunder of it filled his ears; the crash of it upon the reef, the mutter of it at sunset the threat on fury of it storms - on every hand wherever he turned - the Sea

Terror of the Sea

It was the Sea that Mafatu feared. He had been surrounded by it ever since he was born. The thunder of it filled his ears; the crash of it upon the reef, the mutter of it at sunset, the threat and fury of its storms - on every hand, wherever he turned - the Sea

Terror of the Sea

It was the Sea that Mafatu feared. He had been surrounded by it ever since he was born. The thunder of it filled his ears; the crash of it upon the reef, the mutter of it at sunset, the threat and fury of its storms - on every hand, wherever he turned - the Sea.

Manchester, 1991/2. Nine-year-old pupils; unlined paper without margins.

Interpreting writing styles

Abbé Jean-Hippolyte Michon, a French priest who is considered the originator of scientific graphology, did exactly that. He collected handwriting samples from hundreds of people he knew well and compared them. Starting from the premise that each sign had a fixed explanation, he drew up a list:

Soft curves with slanted writing = willingness.
Angled writing with straight lines = severity.
Forceful 't' bars = will-power.

and so on. In 1872 his book *Les Mystères de l'Ecriture* (The Mysteries of Writing) was published, the first of many.

Michon's contribution to handwriting analysis was quite impressive – he coined the word 'graphology' and formulated a law of balance, which stressed that interpretations should be blended. But his system was flawed and its acceptance caused confusion. His assumption that each sign indicates a single character trait is too simplistic and leads to wrong conclusions. If it were true, analysing handwriting would be like doing calculations: you would take the characteristics of a person's writing, compare them with the list of meanings in the book and add the two together to arrive at the character traits.

Modern transparent measuring device used by graphologists.

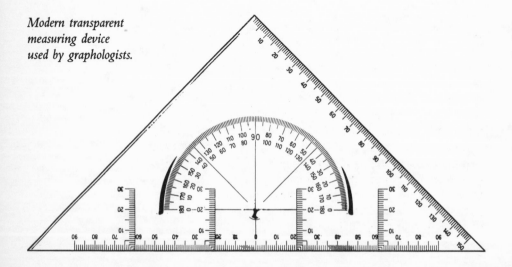

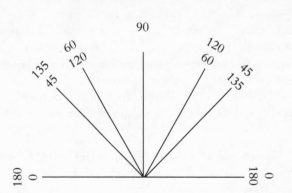

Eugen Schwiedland's Graphometer (Die Graphologie, 1883).

The nineteenth century produced other pragmatic thinkers: in 1882 a German, Eugen Schwiedland, designed his Graphometer, a kind of protractor for the measurement of temperament from the angle of handwriting slant. He wrote in his book *Die Graphologie* (Graphology) that 100 degrees = unnaturalness; 90 degrees = coldness; 70 degrees = a warm emotional life; 50 degrees = an almost passionate temperament; 30 degrees = over-sensitivity; and 10 degrees = emotional illness — hysterics.

Pinpointing character traits

To wriggle character traits into a scheme like this obviously has great disadvantages — everything becomes white or black. In fact, the writing angle means different things in different writing.

It was not long before this fact was established as an important principle in handwriting analysis. A French psychologist, Jean Crepieux-Jamin, began to set graphology on a scientific basis by classifying writing features into speed, pressure, direction, continuity, arrangement, form and dimension. He concluded that such characteristics had to be seen in terms of their interrelationships, and published his findings in a famous book *L'Ecriture et le Caractère* (Writing and Character, 1888).

It is now accepted that just as one note does not make a tune, one graphological oddity does not constitute a character trait; several are needed to draw a firm conclusion about the personality and character of the writer. People are made up of traits in a dynamic cohesion: they link together like the parts of an ever-changing jigsaw puzzle, to reveal the whole personality. So, over many years, handwriting analysts have learned that a handwriting characteristic is only significant in connection with others in the sample, and to draw conclusions only from those characteristics that manifest themselves as written traits.

That is why, when analysing handwriting, you must follow the practice suggested in 1625 by Camillo Baldi, a physician and Professor of Philosophy at the University of Bologna in Italy. In his treatise on how to recognize the character of writers from their letter formations, he observed that 'loose notes are not as suitable for judgement as the whole letter'. What Baldi was saying was that analysis should begin with an enquiry into the extent and origins of the sample.

To make an analysis you need a sample of uninhibited, natural writing. You should therefore start by enquiring whether the sample was written in a natural way or under special circumstances. And the sample should be sizeable. Although one letter of 15 to 20 lines is adequate and will provide the basis for a reliable report by an experienced analyst, several letters, written over a period of time, are even more useful. Temporary influences will show up more clearly if you did not spot them in the first place.

People were analysing handwriting long before graphology was recognized as a subject for academic study. In the eighteenth century, the German philosopher and writer Johann Wolfgang von Goethe wrote that handwriting, like body movement, is an expression of individuality. Edgar Allan Poe, the nineteenth-century American writer of mystery and horror stories, and the French novelist George Sand, Chopin's mistress, analysed handwritten manuscripts. Many scientists felt by intuition that handwriting could tell them much about human character. Among them was the eighteenth-century German scientist Johann Kaspar Lavater, whose theory of physiognomy (the art of judging character from features) was influential in Victorian England.

But what was obviously needed was a theory to explain the connection, and some rational proof.

Mouth, foot and brain-writing

The explanations and proof that established the validity of handwriting analysis appeared with a flurry of interest in the subject in the late nineteenth century. In 1895, Wilhelm Preyer, Professor of Psychiatry and Physiology at Jena in

Germany, made the important discovery that people who had lost the use of their hands — such as soldiers who had been wounded in battle — could learn to write using their mouth or a foot. And when they did so, they wrote in the same style, with the same characteristics, as when they used to write with their hands.

He published his findings in *Zur Psychologie des Schreibens* (On the Psychology of Writing) in 1895, and in several subsequent books. Clearly, he concluded, the term 'handwriting' is a misnomer. The mechanical act of writing is governed by the conscious part of the brain; but the way an individual writes is also guided by the unconscious mind. 'Brainwriting' would be a more accurate description.

What happens in the brain during writing activity was first understood by a German psychiatrist, Dr George Meyer, in Berlin at the turn of the century. He looked at the handwriting of manic depressive patients in a psychiatric hospital and published the results in 1901 in his book *Die Wissenschaftliche Grundlagen der Graphologie* (The Scientific Basis of Graphology).

He found that when his patients were in the excited and happy phase of their illness, a strong impulse towards movement was generated. This caused their writing to become larger, quicker and wider, and the lines would ascend. When they were depressed, however, every movement cost effort, and the writing would become smaller, slower and show less pressure, while the lines would descend.

Dr Meyer realized that the impulses that generate writing travel directly from the brain along the nerves that cause the muscles to work, just as they do to generate walking or running. In writing, the impulses generate a series of refined and complicated hand movements, and it is these tiny movements that register the influences of the unconscious mind.

Writing movements engage the mind in much the same way as walking does — you can distinguish different people by their gestures and body movements, just as you can distinguish them by their different writing. Observing body movements tells you whether a person is vain, insecure, inhibited or self-assured. Writing movements are immensely more detailed; the pen registers the slightest oscillation. Handwriting can tell you much more.

Black and white

Like scientists, handwriting experts have to balance objectivity and subjectivity in their analyses. Too little objective thinking can impede progress by taking a diversion into the realms of fantasy. On the other hand, subjectivity is often transformed into creativity, and too little might mean missing those sudden flashes of inspiration — the 'Eureka element' — which enable long leaps forward. Doctors have to use subjective judgement frequently; particle physicists rely on it. It also plays an important part in handwriting analysis.

To the division of handwriting features into pressure, direction and so on, Professor Ludwig Klages, a German chemist and psychologist, introduced a new concept. He called it *Formniveau*. In English, the literal translation would be 'form level', but what the term is intended to convey is 'level of liveliness, originality, individuality, pure rhythm'. Klages developed this concept to help people judge a very subjective aspect of handwriting: the overall impression of a person's script.

'Form level' is a rather offputting term in English, and it is commonly misunderstood by students of graphology, because they take the word 'form' to mean 'shape' — its primary definition. In fact, the word 'form' has many meanings; in Klages' philosophy the term 'form level' is linked to 'purity' and the general standard of personality.

Klages distinguished five form levels in handwriting: very low, low, average, high and very high. He judged a script's form level low when it is slack, impersonal, banal and unrhythmic. (He regarded lack of originality, schoolish copybook style and banality as neglect of form.) In unrhythmic script, the spaces between words do not give the impression of natural pauses, so the words are spread irregularly over the writing space, and the lines mingle (the descending strokes run into the letters in the line below). A script's form level is high when the writing is natural, original, lively and rhythmic, the distances between the words are about equal, and the lines are separated. In good form level writing, there is a pleasing spatial balance between black and white on the page.

Klages based his system on a simple idea: each writing feature can be explained in two different ways, both valid, but not equally so — one is positive and one is negative.

He underpinned this theory with the idea that every human action can originate from either of two reasons: you can do something on an impulse or an urge, or not do it out of inhibition; you might do something because you are uninhibited, or not do it because the urge is weak. It follows that there are two possible interpretations of every writing feature, because a movement can originate from either of two contradictory tendencies.

Klages supported these ideas with examples from his practice. Narrow writing, for instance, can be the result of self-discipline, so positive. But it also has a negative interpretation, indicating distrust or narrow-mindedness. Calm and controlled conduct can be rooted in self-discipline, so be positive. But it can also result from lack of liveliness constraining will-power and decisiveness, and so be negative. Which of the two interpretations to apply depends on the interrelationship between the many different features in the writing, and especially on the form level.

Following Klages' system, once the form level is determined, you can evaluate other characteristics of the writing in a positive or negative light. Thus, a regular, rhythmic script, classified as high form level, might be judged positive if other characteristics in the script indicate will-power (the writer exercises self-control); or negative if it is too regular and other characteristics give an impression of rigidity and lack of feeling (the writer is insensitive). The highest form level allows a positive evaluation of handwriting characteristics; the lowest level a negative one. Klages drew up comprehensive graded charts of the meaning of individual signs in writing, in which their ambiguity is brought out.

Klages was a system-builder, and to his theories of form level and positive and negative values, he added two others: rhythm (summarized above) and guiding image. This postulates that writers subconsciously want their handwriting to represent their self-image.

Klages was a highly gifted graphologist, thorough and strongly analytical. His most important work, *Handschrift und Charakter* (Handwriting and Character, 1917) was reprinted many times, influencing the thinking of generations of graphologists. His works have been translated into many languages. But, like any attempt to produce an all-embracing system of thought, Klages' theories had their limitations. His concept of positive and negative was underpinned by a deep-rooted anti-Semitism and a philosophy of the struggle between good and evil, whereby the Jew was an instrument of destruction, not a human being, his human face a mask. By 'purity', Klages meant ethnic, racial purity. He never repudiated these ideas, but confirmed them in 1954, two years before his death and well after the Holocaust. His way of thinking was a gift to the Nazis.[1]

Less agile minds solidified Klages' ideas into a system of extremes and certainties, black and white. An over-adherence to rules overshadowed German research and progress for a time. Nevertheless, Klages' towering personality contributed much to the body of knowledge about handwriting, and his legacy of the awareness of positive and negative interpretation greatly furthered handwriting analysis.

The psychology behind handwriting

In its broadest sense, psychology deals with and encompasses many schools of thought. Some are generally regarded as spurious, or at best quasi-scientific, because they do not incorporate true scientific observation and principles. You can see from what you have read so far that graphology, as described in this book, focuses specifically on psychology in the analytical/emotional sense. In other words, it follows the tradition of Freud, Jung, Adler, Erickson, Piaget and others. Its objective is to discover the hidden emotional condition of the subject, as it is portrayed in that person's handwriting. An understanding of basic psychology will be useful, therefore, in helping you develop the skill of handwriting analysis.

The best place to begin is with a basic model of the psyche depicting the 'normal' state of awareness in a healthy human being (*see* overleaf). It shows the consciousness, the unique 'organism' within all of us, which is totally aware of what is happening to and around us.

The unconscious

It is easiest to understand the unconscious if you think of it as an assemblage of all the known dynamic elements of personality, plus the unknown elements. These are hidden energies of a different mental order from those of the conscious, which they modify and influence in all sorts of ways. They harbour complex psychic energies in great variety.

[1] For fascinating and scholarly detail, see pp.9–46 of 'Das graphologische System Ludwig Klages' by Ursula Avé-Lallemand in *Die vier deutschen Schulen der Graphologie* (E. Reinhardt, Munich, 1989).

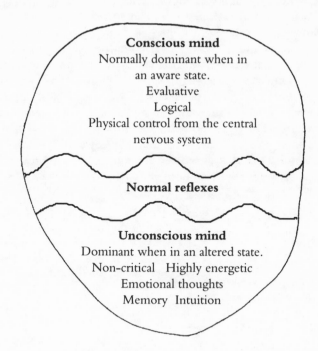

The conscious mind is normally the more dominant, in the sense that it is logically orientated, and responsible for motor (central) control of the body. For example, powers of speech are operated from the conscious. The conscious mind also evaluates the complex messages it receives continually from within the self, as well as from the outer world.

By contrast, the functions of the unconscious mind are wholly uncritical, but highly energetic. This becomes obvious when you wake up from a nightmare. This is because the unconscious deals with emotions, which may change radically: from fear to hate, from anger to love and joy.

The unconscious mind is imaginative and intuition stems from its deepest recesses. In an altered state of consciousness, such as hypnosis, a person's handwriting during regression back to childhood will reflect the state of mind arrived at during the hypnosis. If a childlike state is recalled, 'automatic handwriting' will be generated by the brain, characteristic of the recalled childhood age.

Psychic energy converts readily to physical energy. For

example, it will provide the power to run or stand and fight if attacked: the 'fight or flight' syndrome.

Dr Roger Walcott Sperry, winner of the Nobel Prize for Medicine in 1981, brought these ideas together through his experiments into the way the brain works. In his 'split brain' concept, Dr Sperry sees the brain as consisting of two distinct lobes connected physiologically by a myriad of nerves, all functioning separately (*see* below). When applied to handwriting, one side of the brain is responsible for how the script is penned. The other provides the material that is written, such as in a job application. Although Sperry's work is highly complex, in that it deals with such a complicated organ as the brain, his basic ideas apply to handwriting analysis.

The Jungian school

This is a good point at which to look at the work of the celebrated Swiss psychologist Carl Gustav Jung and the Jungian school of psychology. One of Jung's famous

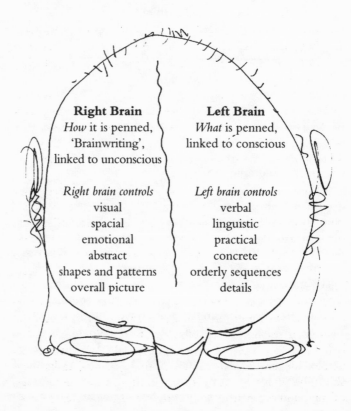

Right Brain
How it is penned,
'Brainwriting',
linked to unconscious

Right brain controls
visual
spacial
emotional
abstract
shapes and patterns
overall picture

Left Brain
What is penned,
linked to conscious

Left brain controls
verbal
linguistic
practical
concrete
orderly sequences
details

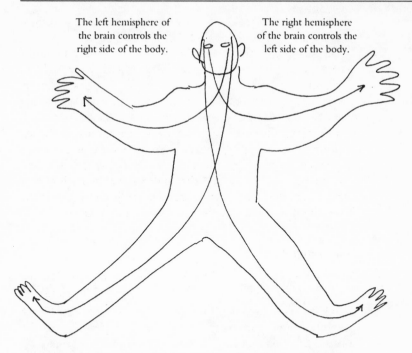

The left hemisphere of the brain controls the right side of the body.

The right hemisphere of the brain controls the left side of the body.

assertions is that all males have some female characteristics and all females have some male ones. Jung claimed that there are no exceptions to this rule, only the degree to which it varies from person to person.

This idea helps explain why both male and female writing shows some of the opposite sex's traits. *Animus* and *anima* are the terms Jung used to emphasize the inner part of the human personality in its communion with the unconscious mind. So Jungian psychology is linked with physiological theories (*see* diagram overleaf).

In practice, a person's strengths and weaknesses are displayed as graphological traits that can be accurately linked with a job specification. For example, personnel officers are often surprised to find in a graphological report for a woman that she displays assertion or aggression in her handwriting and may possess the very qualities necessary for a forceful sales representative.

Recent scientific evidence indicates that sex differences are biological in origin: the brains of men and women differ as a result of sex hormones. Already at an early age, boys are better at target-directed motor skills, while girls have greater verbal fluency and can carry out some manual tasks more skillfully. This may mean there will never be equal numbers of men and women in some professions; however, in both

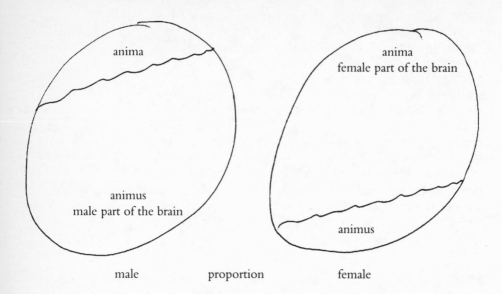

male   proportion   female

sexes the range of ability is wide and most professions require a blend of skills that can be provided in more than one way.

In the USA there is an enormous interest in psychology. Its popularity has been fuelled by a business community quick to recognize its huge potential for personnel selection, and its application for deeper understanding of people and the qualities that motivate them. The American psychologist Milton Erickson brought many psychological theories together, so popularizing them. It was only one step further to Vance Packard and his work *The Hidden Persuaders*. The figure opposite shows physiological perception of the workings of the mind.

The Freudian school

The model opposite is based largely on mid-European influences. It helps explain the psychoanalyst school of Sigmund Freud. At the centre is the ego, a person's self-perception, or, as Freud noted, 'the dynamic unity of self which is in direct touch with external reality'. Protecting this highly sensitive area of the mind is the persona, functioning as a mask for the outside world.

Jung employed the term 'persona' to express 'the function complex which determines an individual's reactions with reference to objective situations'. The handwritten script represents the ego in the fullest sense and the signature the persona, the front or mask. It is interesting how signatures often differ from the signers' ordinary handwriting.

The super ego designates that area of the unconscious that is built up by early experiences. This is based on a child's reactions to its parents or carers. It becomes the conscience, criticizing the thoughts and acts stemming from the ego, thus creating feelings of guilt and anxiety.

The Freudian school of psychology coined the term 'id' to express the earliest basic drives: the primitive, instinctive, urgent forces and energies in humans. These are the animalistic elements: the desire for survival, self-preservation, protection, shelter. In the id, the drives, gut feelings and energies stemming from the unconscious mind are embodied. If the ego tries to gratify certain impulses, the id may, in an unharmonious person, lead to further disharmony.

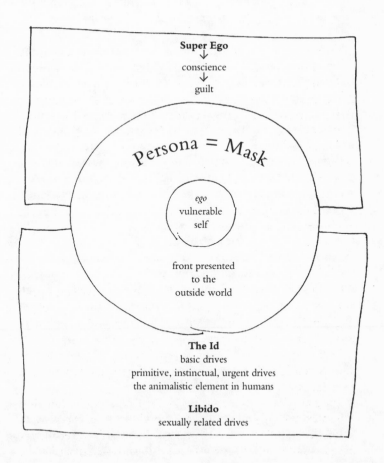

The symbolism of space

The graphologist recognizes hundreds of signs within a person's handwriting that tie up with these models of the mind. Early in the twentieth century the Swiss psychologist Dr Max Pulver applied the findings of Freud and Jung directly to graphology. He theorized that individual expression in handwriting is based on symbolism emerging from archetypes (mental images) hidden in the depths of the psyche. He widened Klages' concepts by realizing that there may, therefore, be not just two but several interpretations of handwriting characteristics. The interpretation depends on the biological and the psychological traits and complexes of the writer. Stubbornness, for example, might be seen by a scientist as a trait likely to promote systematic ongoing thought, by a sales manager as a guarantee of ultimate success, and by a cleric as a danger leading to collision with people and feelings. Pulver termed this concept 'existential quality'.

Pulver developed Klages' ideas on form level in his concept of *Wesensart*, literally 'individual essence' or 'amalgam of body and spirit of the self'. He defines this as a totality of the physical, mental, and spiritual peculiarities of the individual. According to Pulver, conscious writing is subconscious drawing, a symbolic projection of the personality. For example, while Klages considers the pressure a writer exercises as an expression of the will, Pulver sees it as a projection from the subconscious. This theory explains why so many people who are engaged in heavy physical work write with light pressure.

Finally, Pulver pioneered the concept of three zones in the formation of letters (*see* p.56 and p.78). Pulver theorized that the upper zone symbolizes abstraction, intellect, spiritual traits, fantasy, imagination and intuition. The middle zone is symbolic of conscious daily life, realism, social self, ego and expression. And the lower zone represents instincts, sexual drive, security, self-preservation, subconscious drives for material demands, well-being and possessions.

Using graphology in business

The application of graphology to business is a new idea to many people in the UK. Yet as early as the 1900s European banker/businessman Siegmund Warburg often had handwriting experts to assist him. His interest in the newly emerging science of psychology led him to perceive the potential for using handwriting analysis in business. Graphology helps us understand psychological connections and find solutions to certain psychological problems. Using graphology daily in his business, Warburg found he could solve problems that seemed insurmountable.

Warburg knew that many people then considered graphologists eccentric, but he considered them pioneers in a new field of psychological knowledge. Many sciences have a past rooted in mythology. Scientific understanding of the universe began as astrology and only in the course of time did the science of astronomy develop from it. No one would call an astronomer eccentric nowadays.

Warburg's experience with graphology convinced him that graphological analysis gives insight into the psychological structure of other people. It enables us to gain a deeper knowledge about them than either spontaneous, intuitive impression or years of personal acquaintance can give. Warburg was convinced by experience that an individual's handwriting shows characteristics that can be interpreted by an experienced graphologist to reveal more than the facial expression, the movements or the verbal declarations of that person would unveil. He was convinced that one day graphology would be considered a source of scientific knowledge, comparable with astronomy, chemistry and physics.

That day has dawned. Graphology, the science — and art — of determining from handwriting the character of the writer, belongs to the field of psychodiagnostics, the science of applied psychology. But that is not the end of the story. Researchers are still tracing the physiological origins of writing to their source in the brain and still mapping its connections with the personality. But, as a result of the discoveries outlined on these pages, they now know that human character is not just a collection of traits, but the potential for action released by the interplay of these traits with the outside world. The rest of this book is an attempt to explain how to release that potential.

2 Fitting the Right Person to the Right Job

Handwriting analysis is the simplest, most unbiased and most unobtrusive personality test available. It is simple because instead of a piecemeal approach, consisting of various unrelated tests, you end up with one holistic report focused on a particular person's suitability for a specified position to be filled. It is unbiased because you gain an objective impression of likely candidates before seeing them at interview. It is unobtrusive because the candidate will not be present while the test is carried out.

A handwriting report should be seen as the primary tool in candidate selection. It will give a plain, factual yet thorough summary of the candidate's suitability for the job advertised. It may be used at any stage in the selection process — before interview, as a second opinion in between interviews, and to assist you in your line and depth of questioning.

The report must also be seen as one link — albeit the central link — in a chain of events by which the right person is fitted to the right job.

A perceptive occupational analysis can only be made on the basis of a good *job specification*. This is the first link in the chain, and the basis for the second link: the *job advertisement*. You, as interviewer, will draw up a shortlist of candidates for consideration from their handwritten applications, or you will have designed a good *application form*, to be filled in by hand by the candidate. That is the third link.

The chain has several more links. On the basis of the handwriting reports, and perhaps a skills test, you will want to call, say, the three or four most likely candidates on your shortlist for *interview*. But the interview, to be objective and informative, must be properly structured. Therefore you need a *check list* of questions to ask at interview. When the candidate has been selected, his or her application and all notes should be filed for future reference. This might be of importance for promotion, salary review or other periodic professional *appraisal and assessment procedure.*

The job specification

A basic job specification is essential to every employer and employee. It provides the basis of the agreement between the company and its staff, and so can be used to resolve problems that may arise during and after employment.

The job specification can also be useful for looking at organizational structure, and clarifying departmental and individual responsibilities. These days, what is called 'function analysis' for financial grading of employees is an integral part of many EC directives. And companies facing arbitration tribunals are advised to carry out job evaluation to ensure equal value for equal jobs, to protect themselves against claims of sex or race discrimination and for other current or future legislation affecting employment.

Most important, however, is the usefulness of the job specification as an aid for fitting the right person to the right job.

Many employers find drawing up a job specification in detail the most difficult part of the job selection process. To get over this hurdle, start with the main elements:

1. Job description and possible titles.
2. Requirements, training or skill level; duties.
3. Purpose of the job.
4. The place of the employee in the organization.
5. Salary and benefits.

Thinking through all these elements will help you to work out the attributes you want the successful candidate to have.

To work out the *purpose of the job*, summarize as briefly as you can the result(s) you ultimately expect from the employee, for example: to increase the number of customers you deal with; to increase the turnover; to handle the East Europe sector; to design marketing material, liaising with the sales department; to be the clients' telephone problem–solver and answer their complaints. This will help you when you come to think of what attributes you want the candidate to have.

If you find it hard to work out *the place of the employee in the organization*, it can be useful to draw a simple tree (see overleaf).

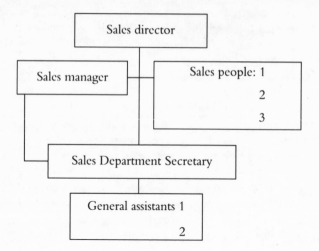

Salary and benefits need to be worked out in detail – this can be a complex process.

The job description needs careful consideration to attract the right applicants. A condensed version will be needed to draw up the job advertisement. A fully specified one will be required as part of the contract of employment. You may find it helpful to start by listing your requirements under different headings, such as necessary skills (*see* example of a skills evaluation chart opposite); personal attributes you think your employees should have (level of education, experience, high motivation, pioneering ability, for example); and character traits specifically needed for the job in question (the ability to work under pressure, perhaps, or a methodical mind). Appendix 3 has lists of personality requirements for different jobs, which may help you with this.

When you have compiled your list, it is a useful exercise to give some thought to exactly what you are thinking of when you use words like 'attitude' and 'personality'. Thousands of words have been written about the precise nature, meaning and definition of these keywords, so it is important to communicate exactly what you mean when you use the word in a job profile. Here are some keywords you are likely to use, and their meanings as applied to the working environment, business, and the professions:

Intelligence

This is a good concept to head your list, since the type of intelligence required for different jobs can be very different,

Skill Evaluation

Name:
Age:
Experience:

Self-appraisal:
Standard achieved:
Standard required:

Key:
● Essential to evaluate
+ Evaluate where appropriate
− Not applicable
Seen by:
Date:

		Word Processor Operators	P.A./S.H. Secretaries and Typists	P.A./ Secretaries no Short-hand	Audio Secretaries and Typists	Phone Sales and/or Client Support Staff	Accounts Wages	Figure Clerks, Data Input VDU	Filing, General, Misc. Clerks	School-leavers, Juniors
Typing evaluation	Speed									
	Tabulation									
	Manuscript									
	Spelling/Layout/ Punctuation									
Shorthand evaluation	80 wpm									
	100 wpm									
	120 wpm									
Word Processing evaluation	Layout									
	Accuracy									
Clerical evaluation	Speed									
	Filing Orderliness									
	Adaptability									
	Numeracy									
Phone evaluation	Manner									
	Voice									
Handwriting evaluation	Fax									
	Notes									

and type of intelligence is an attribute that can be determined from a handwriting sample.

A useful definition of intelligence is: the ability to acquire knowledge and then solve problems with this knowledge. However, some jobs need an intelligence that is able to generate ideas, while others need intelligence coupled to speed of decision, when a quick resolution may be called for. There is abstract intelligence, derived from reasoning, required for the resolution of concrete, perhaps technical, problems; and fluid intelligence, needed for the creative solution of novel problems.

To help you pinpoint which aspect of intelligence you want your candidate to have, here is a list from which you can select the right combination of attributes:

1. Speedy understanding based on the ability to combine abstract thought with experience and acquired knowledge.
2. The ability to observe and memorize, and to profit from experience. (This does not necessarily coincide with the type of intelligence measured by intelligence tests.)
3. The quality of abstraction, objectivity, learning and dealing with novelty.
4. The ability to conceptualize effectively and to grasp relationships.
5. The ability to reduce complex matters swiftly to their essence and see them in perspective, in order to draw useful conclusions.
6. A general ability displayed in performing a wide variety of tasks in differing circumstances.
7. The combination of natural intellectual ability and acquired knowledge/experience.
8. Indigenous brainpower displayed in the successful solution of daily and long-term problems.

Personality

Every person is uniquely different from every other, so personality may be defined as an individual's characteristic pattern of more or less enduring behaviour and thought, as distinct from those of others. Personality is therefore a concept derived from behaviour and so is observable. Consider a personality trait such as persistence. However, our different personality strands and traits are not *always* static; they function like a pack of cards, constantly being shuffled and played in our reaction to outside factors.

The personality you describe must be compatible with your job description. Draw up a list of personal qualities (consistent, project-orientated, long-term thinker and so on) that match the job.

Ability

This may be defined as the capacity for skilful performance, usually on an already learned task. Checking academic and professional qualifications, and taking up appropriate references, will obviously serve to determine candidates' knowledge and previous experience for positions requiring them. However, you may also want to know about candidates' abilities in other directions. For example:

- *Communications skills:* the ability to impart and convey knowledge, ideas and instructions freely and clearly, so that the recipient is left with an accurate understanding of what is meant. A good communicator shares information and leaves the door open for response. A clear, articulated voice and legible handwriting helps.
- *Interpersonal relations:* the abundance or lack of the social skills required to deal successfully at work and at leisure with others, be they equals, superiors or subordinates. The manner in which a person interacts with other people.
- *Job performance:* a combination of attitude and functional skills displayed in relation to required job standards. The tendency of employers to want to get rid of an employee whose job performance is not up to standard is the reason why references are so often unrevealing. Handwriting analysis will uncover negative attitude problems and the report will show whether a person has, for example, the patience to carry out detailed work successfully.
- *Executive skills:* the ability to translate ideas and plans into effective action. Administrative and leadership qualities, coupled with the ability to inspire, motivate and delegate, applied to operating a business. Qualities needed for a general manager are listed on p.174.

Aptitude

Ability and aptitude differ in that the latter is the capacity to master a *new* job, and skilful or artful performance on an as yet *unlearned* task. A person with the right aptitude for a job shows clear creative abilities in that direction.

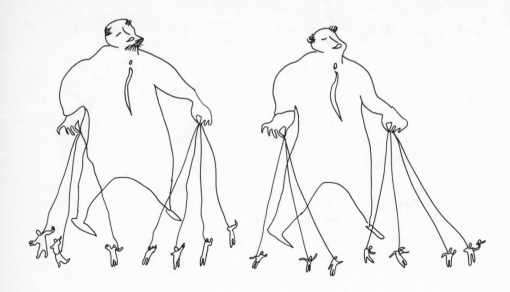

Attitude

1. *Towards work:* independence; energy; initiative; perseverance; organizational ability; business acumen; response to pressure; responsibility; loyalty.
2. *Towards others:* communications skills; powers of persuasion; authority; tact; team spirit.

Creativity

When applied to a work situation, creativity is:

1. The seeking and discovering of new relationships and new solutions to (old or new) problems;
2. Mental processes that lead to solutions; ideas; conceptualization, artistic forms, theories or products that are unique and novel.

Motivation

Self-motivation is the desire to accomplish, the ability to act without prompting in order to achieve superior results. However, some people respond to:

Motivation by incentive, i.e. external activity stimuli for competitive, materialistic gain, prestige, love of the limelight or power.

Reliability

Dependable, supportive, predictable behaviour with consistent effort.

Emotional maturity

The capacity to understand and deal with one's own impulses and feelings, as well as others' motives and responses to them.

Other character traits often requested by employers are listed in Appendix 3.

To complete your job specification, grade each item on your list according to a scale of importance (for example: essential; very important; useful). Also indicate any qualities you consider undesirable. Such a list will be useful as an *aide-mémoire* at interview and for apportioning weight when analysing the applicant's handwriting, and it will help you in writing out the job description. A sample job specification is overleaf.

The job advertisement

Advertising is expensive, so the wording needs to be short and to the point. Refer to the items listed under 'necessary skills' and the character traits designated 'essential' in the list, and mention those first: 'The successful candidate must have experience in selling fast-moving consumer goods to multiples. Must be adaptable and capable of negotiating long-term contracts with top management.'

You may prefer to ask for a handwriting sample at this stage: 'Please reply in your own handwriting, enclosing a typed c.v.' or something similar.

The application form

Besides the handwritten letter of application (*see above*), you may use an application form which should be headed 'Use own handwriting throughout'. This should ensure enough handwriting for an accurate analysis. The analyst should ideally receive the equivalent of one side of an A4 sheet of handwriting and needs a minimum of 15 to 20 lines, with a

Job Specification

POSITION   — Market Researcher/Analyst
SALARY   — Negotiable up to £................ pa + bonus
JOB PURPOSE   — To assist the Marketing Director in creating a new
                Department.

Main Duties

With a multi-disciplined approach the main duties are likely to include:

1. Analytical research work in-house with some site visits
2. Identifying new markets and developing existing ones
3. In-house reporting
4. Preparing a selection of projects
5. Maintaining a library of journals and magazines
6. Maintaining files on competitors' information and newspaper cuttings of interest
7. Product Management

Essential Requirements

1. A degree in Marketing
2. 1–2 years' work experience in the Marketing field is preferable but not essential
3. Persistent, with good attention to detail, flexible, methodical, analytical, numerate and a good communicator. Sense of responsibility. Keen. Self starter.
4. Experience in computer operations and word processing.

Benefits

1. Good career opportunities to progress to Product or Marketing Manager
2. The challenge of working in a small company where initiative is applauded and the future depends on performance. The complete satisfaction of seeing a marketing concept develop all the way to product launch
3. An attractive salary with profit-related bonus
4. Further specialist marketing and management training

signature. Leave plenty of broad, unlined spaces on the application form to allow the candidate freedom of expression, so that there is enough text to analyse.

If the candidate was educated abroad, it will be useful for the analyst to know where the candidate learned to write. This is a question you could ask at first interview if it is not clear on the c.v.

Print a declaration at the bottom of the form requiring a signature, for example: 'I declare that the information given in this application form is correct and I understand that if I am appointed by the Company, the appointment will be subject to acceptance of the Company's employment policy.'

Do remember to ask for the names of referees somewhere on the application form.

There are several advantages in obtaining a handwritten application before interviewing. It will save you valuable time. You can cut down the number of candidates to interview by quickly separating those who do not fulfil the requirements from the most likely applicants.

It is a good idea to interview each candidate briefly by telephone to produce a shortlist of three to five likely people per vacancy. Their letters should then be analysed. Until you feel confident enough to make your own analyses it would be sensible to produce your own written reports and compare them with the professional reports.

The practices described above make it less likely that you will allow yourself to be influenced by subjective factors at interview and you start with a clear image of suitable candidates from an objective handwriting analysis.

If you have not obtained a handwritten letter and/or application form, you might ask each candidate for one before or during an interview. For example, you might supply an A4 sheet and a ballpoint pen, and ask the candidates to explain what contribution they could bring to the advertised job. How could their past experience and strengths be successfully applied? The idea is to give them a question that will make them think, so that they are not concentrating on the writing, which should be as natural as possible.

The interview

The foregoing links in the chain can be thought of as the recruitment phase; next comes the selection phase. Most employers select from interview. Indeed, interviewing is the eternal test, as old as employment. In spite of widespread scepticism and prophesies about its eclipse (but little about what might replace it), the interview refuses to die, because it is natural for people to want to see for themselves and get a feeling for a person. Psychometric tests may well be used to try to quantify aspects of personality, but in the end you know you have to work with people in their totality. The personal chemistry in a team is as important as ever. The interview is and will remain the most widely used DIY selection tool.

It is not the task of this book to investigate interviewing techniques, but rather to make one main observation: an interview will never be fully informative or successful if it is not structured — that is, the interviewer(s) must work out in advance what they want to know. For this it is necessary to refer to the job requirements, duties and benefits (*see* p.48), and to draw up an interview check list, detailing what you, as interviewer, want to know and need to explain.

The interview check list

If you follow these guidelines you can be sure at the end of the interview that your picture of the candidate is as complete as possible. They will help you to observe each candidate as thoroughly as time allows, and will help to keep your impressions objective.

1. Go through the details given on the c.v., and note on your check list any missing information, anything you would like to know more about, and so on.

2. Biographical information
   Leave a space under this heading to add details about:

   • the candidate's place in the family
   • family vocational traditions
   • achievements to date
   • career development plans
   • self-image

   Such background details will assist judgement about present suitability, chances of future progress and how the candidate will fit into the company culture.

3. List the qualities you decided are required or undesirable when drawing up the job description (*see* Appendix 2).

Personality Traits Employers' Request

Criteria		Excellent	Above Average	Average	Below Average	Poor
Initiative	1.					
Independence	2.					
Problem–analysis	3.					
Decision-making & judgement	4.					
Persuasiveness	5.					
Interpersonal skills	6.					
Planning & organizing skills	7.					
Adaptability	8.					
Flexibility	9.					
Tenacity	10.					
Total						

Include in the list intelligence, personality, attitude towards work and attitude towards others. You can then evaluate the candidate accordingly and compare your observations with the graphological findings.

4. Add any points for further investigation thrown up by the handwriting analysis report.

5. Make a note to remember to obtain details about the candidate's health and record of absence from work.

6. Add a final heading: 'general appearance'. Note under it the candidate's tidiness and other general impressions, such as degree of friendliness, ability to listen, tendency to interrupt, sense of humour, sound of voice, body language, and so on.

7. Leave a space at the bottom of the form in which to record the candidate's questions.

If you leave space on the form to write notes as the interview progresses, the form can be filed as a useful record for future reference.

After the interview there remains only the checking of references and any practical tests, before the final decision. Do not be satisfied with written references; contact the referees by phone and dig deep. Be specific — for example, ask for the absence record, frequency of illness and recurring complaints, any record concerning cheating, drink or drug problems.

Annual assessment

Many companies following a policy of training and investing in people now monitor and guide their employees' careers. The monitoring process involves recording their annual performance and achievements on an assessment form.

In case you find inconsistencies or significant changes in the employees' performance it may be worthwhile reappraising the candidate by handwriting analysis. The same applies if significant promotion is considered. Although you do not need to ask the permission of candidates who apply for an advertised job before analysing their handwriting, for re-appraisal it is important to obtain the employees' permission. It would be unethical for a graphologist to carry out an analysis of an employee's handwriting without the writer's permission, unless the analysis were part of an investigation of some kind. You, as an amateur graphologist, must adhere to the same principles.

You can adapt for your own use the sample Yearly Assessment Form shown opposite.

Following this procedure as outlined, using the lists and sample forms in this chapter will ensure that you:

- Select better-researched personnel, closely matched to the position and duties.
- Achieve higher staff retention, resulting in lower recruitment costs, more effective training results and more consistent productivity.
- Gain valuable psychological insight into the people you employ, enabling you to motivate and direct your personnel resources more effectively.

Yearly Assessment Form

✓ Employee Self-Assessment
○ Manager Assessment
+ Handwriting Analysis
Date:
Manager:

Employee: Age:
Dept:
Years of Service:
Position:
Health/days off: =   %

1.	*Knowledge of Work:* Having the technical and administrative skills and knowledge required for this position.	Has exceptional knowledge of own and related work.	Has required job-related knowledge.	Needs instruction or guidance.	
		5 4	3 2	1	
2.	*Initiative, Resourcefulness* Ability to originate ideas and to get things started.	Imaginative and unusually resourceful.	Has average initiative. Meets requirements.	Rarely has new ideas. Lacks imagination.	
		5 4	3 2	1	
3.	*Application and Drive, Commitment* Attention and application to work. Self-motivation. Time management.	Exceptionally industrious. Highly self-motivated.	Steady and willing worker.	Wastes time. Needs close supervision.	
		5 4	3 2	1	
4.	*Quality of Work, Pressure Resistance* Thoroughness, neatness and accuracy of work.	Consistently maintains highest quality.	Regularly meets recognized standards.	Needs improvement.	
		5 4	3 2	1	
5.	*Volume of Work* Quantity of acceptable work. Measurable results.	Unusually high output and results.	Regularly meets recognized standards.	Less than acceptable. Must be increased.	
		5 4	3 2	1	
6.	*Communications, verbal/in writing* Ability to keep manager/colleagues informed as appropriate.	Very effective communicator.	Generally effective communicator.	Needs substantial improvement.	
		5 4	3 2	1	
7.	*Dealings with Co-Workers, Empathy* Ability to operate constructively with fellow workers and others.	Highly regarded. Advice sought out by others.	Works well with others.	Has difficulty getting along with others.	
		5 4	3 2	1	
8.	*Dependability, Persistence* Reliability in following instructions and carrying out assignments speedily and effectively.	Exceptionally reliable on all assignments.	Dependable on most assignments.	Requires more than normal follow-up.	
		5 4	3 2	1	
9.	*Team Contribution* Contribution to the success of the team or sub-group.	Voluntary high level of contribution.	Participates effectively within group.	Loner. Stays outside team.	
		5 4	3 2	1	
10.	*Timekeeping/Attendance* Reliability of timekeeping, attendance, health.	Timekeeping/ attendance reliable.	Timekeeping/ attendance average.	Timekeeping/ attendance unreliable.	
		5 4	3 2	1	
11.	*Ability to Learn, Aptitude* Ability to master new instructions/ methods. Ability to retain new knowledge.	Exceptionally quick to learn.	Average ability to learn.	Has difficulty grasping new ideas.	
		5 4	3 2	1	
12.	*Memory*	Excellent memory.	Average memory.	Forgetful.	
		5 4	3 2	1	

Notes:

3 Graphology as a Key to Personality and Job Aptitude

Body language plays an important role in our perception of other people. We recognize them from the way they move; their gestures influence our reactions. The pen moves in line with the character of the writer, forcing the personality out on to the paper in movements full of symbolism. The German pioneer of graphology, Ludwig Klages (*see* p.30), says that every psychic happening expresses itself in movements of the body. Movements connected with sadness go down; those connected with happiness go up. Similarly, the lines of an optimistic writer tend to go up, while those of the pessimistic person often slope downward. Our daily language is also full of symbolism: 'over the moon', 'down the drain', 'riding high', 'feeling low', 'downhearted', 'upbeat', 'ups and downs'.

The positioning of line and colour signify the painter filling a canvas — a symbol of living space — in his or her individual way. Script and words symbolize the writer filling a page, signifying empty space. Our written language developed from drawing a picture, simplifying it to a symbol, then to an abstract set of letters far removed from their origin.

The pen of a spontaneous, easily adaptable character moves differently across the page from that of the unbending disciplinarian, whose rigidity will show in stiff, regimented writing. Isolated, lonely people who keep their distance from other people will leave large distances between words. Dynamic, powerful people will not write like mice. Up and down, left and right, tension and release, inhibition and vigour — all are there on the page.

The twentieth-century Swiss graphologist, Dr Max Pulver (*see* p.55), points out that script has very little third dimension. The layer of ink is very thin. Even heavy writing pressure makes only a slight indent. Writing should therefore be considered a flat, two-dimensional form.

However, by instinct, we place it in space, speaking of

I look forward to

Dynamic, powerful men will not write like mice.

Why should I give in? I am not the one who is wrong. I am right.

Sharp edges, not an easy-going character. Ascending line direction.

and offers a reasonable high return and/or capital these facilities should be lightly

Large distances between words. Descending lines.

'upright' or 'backward-slanting' writing, and of 'ascending' or 'descending' lines. We place a dot 'after' a word, or 'above' a stroke, as if it were a body rising above the paper with distance around it. Instead of the two-dimensional writing paper, we perceive a three-dimensional world, writing set in space. Children possess that spatial feeling when they paint a flower or the family on flat paper. They do not need to hold the paper up to bring it closer to the real situation.

Up and down, high and low, light and dark play a great role in the cultural development of human beings. We speak of high moral fibre and a high level of intelligence, and talk about the depths of despair, a dark chapter in history. Our total being, conscious and unconscious, is projected into our handwriting in the form of symbolism.

Handwriting, then, is a collection of graphic symbols, capable of interpretation. Every feature — the slant of letters, their size, the lengths of upstrokes and downstrokes — has symbolic meaning.

The symbolism of space

According to Dr Max Pulver we recognize an imaginary middle line, the border between up and down, the division between day and night. Above are the heavens, the sky, the sun, the day, the light, the spiritual. Below are darkness, the night, depth and the abyss.

Similarly, our letters and words can be divided into three symbolic zones. The idea originated centuries ago, when people were nearer to nature. The zones correspond with natural life-forms, for example, the leaves, trunk and roots of a tree — three in one, from the ancient concept of spirit, soul and body. This trichotomy, assimilated and refined by modern psychology, becomes a point of departure for our observation and analysis of handwriting.

The symbolism of the vertical writing space

Pen movement: up and down

The Three Zones
Upper (UZ), Middle (MZ) and Lower Zone (LZ)

MZ

The sphere of
Forces of reality.
Coping with actuality.
Emotional and social
behaviour.

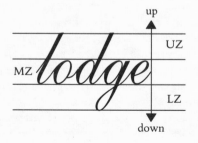

UZ

The sphere of
Mental, spiritual,
abstract forces.

LZ

The sphere of
Material needs.
Psychic and physical
energy. Instinctual
urges.

Letters extending into the Upper Zone – UZ	*Higher Consciousness*
'b', 'd', 'f', 'h', 'k', 'l', 't'	Intellectual, spiritual, ethical, religious ideas; imagination; fantasy. Abstract forces.

Letters in the Middle Zone only – MZ (without UZ or LZ extensions)	*The Conscious*
'a', 'c', 'e', 'i', 'm', 'n', 'o', 'r', 's', 'u', 'v', 'w', 'x', 'z'	Realism, the practical, feeling, social self, egoism/altruism, conscious inner life.

Letters extending into the Lower Zone – LZ	*The Sub or Unconscious*
'f', 'g', 'j', 'p', 'q', 'y', ('z')	Instinctive drives, the material, physical, erotic/sexual urges; formation of collective symbols.

All letters have thus a middle zone, *some* have an upper zone extension, *some* have a lower zone extension.

'f' is the only letter covering the three zones.

'z' is sometimes taught with lower zone extension.

Left-right symbolism: the horizontal writing space

Pen movement: from left to right

This important aspect of symbolism is expressed in many ways in handwriting — the slant of letters, the position of a signature. We write from the left — the symbolic place of the Self; and we go to the right, the Other, the goal, the future. Movements to the right in script go away from our body and are symbolic of the outward-directedness of the writer. Contrary movement to the left in writing, towards the body, symbolizes return to the past and inward-directedness.

UZ
MZ
LZ

The horizontal movement in space.

The horizontal writing movement

LEFT ◄─────────────────────────────► RIGHT

The past, origin,
the Mother breast,
the I or me,
introversion

The future, goal,
the Father hunter,
the Other, you,
extraversion

Rightward movement.

Leftward movement.

And because the mind is a collection of contradictory tendencies, every symbol it projects has many meanings — so it follows that each writing characteristic can have several meanings, both positive and negative.

The way a candidate enters a room, the way she moves her hands, the way he seats himself on his chair — all these gestures tell a story. They might betray nervousness and insecurity or they might indicate confidence and receptiveness. It all depends on how you interpret them. To decide, you must observe closely, considering the candidate's facial expression, and the way he or she answers questions. You should also look at the candidate's gestures in the context of the impression of the person as a whole.

Similarly, when interpreting handwriting, you can attach a meaning to each characteristic only when you have considered its many possible interpretations and looked at it in the context of the other handwriting features and its general appearance.

Recording an impression

First impressions count. This truism relates as much to handwriting — personality expressed graphically — as it does to people. So the first thing to do when starting to analyse handwriting is to look at it and register an impression of its overall appearance.

To record a subjective impression in a meaningful way, you need a way of appraising the elements of the handwriting. To do this, we apply a concept called 'intrinsic value' (I.V.), a term originally used in banking and now adopted in commerce and accountancy, especially in the USA. Very simply, 'intrinsic value' describes the value of something over and above its face, or monetary, value. Applied to graphology, intrinsic value is a concept that we use to appraise the quality of a person's handwriting from its overall impression and certain measurable features.

In the USA the term has a wider meaning than is generally accepted in the UK. According to *Webster's New Collegiate Dictionary*, the term 'intrinsic' does not only include the measurable assets of a company or an object, but also 'the aspects that cannot be measured, but nevertheless apply to the essence, or the essential nature or constitution of a thing'. One can speak of the intrinsic worth of a gem, for example, and we can deal with the intrinsic value of handwriting, its essential quality.

Handwriting is made up of many features you can easily measure — the size of a capital letter, for example, or the angle of a stroke; and features that can be considered to have a purely subjective value — your impression of the rhythm and balance of a script, for example, or the pleasing distribution of white and black on the page. Using the concept of intrinsic value, you can distinguish the aesthetic elements of a handwriting sample (spacing, proportion, rhythm and so on), compare them with the same elements in other handwriting samples and try to appraise each element on the basis of comparison. In handwriting analysis, intrinsic value (I.V.) is the sum total of the tangible and intangible assets of handwriting.

You can see from this that you will only be able to appraise a sample of handwriting — in other words, assess its intrinsic value — when you have carefully compared the elements of many samples. It takes time and experience to become objective and accurate.

Assessing intrinsic value (I.V.)

The first rule of handwriting analysis is: do not start to read a handwriting sample, or study its contents, before first considering its general appearance. Gaining a first impression — and *retaining* it for future reference — is all-important.

Choose a time and a place where you can concentrate and are unlikely to be interrupted. Work seated comfortably at a desk or table in a good light. You will need a copy of our Check List (see p.130). Your other requirements are: a few sheets of paper for notes; a pen; a pencil; two magnifying glasses, one for large areas and a stronger one for small details, the two capable of being superimposed if necessary; a transparent ruler; and a transparent protractor. At a later stage, for specialist jobs, you may require a zoom microscope and a safe for valuable or confidential papers.

Relax and concentrate, but before you start, take the writing sample and give it and your Check List — and your notes — the same reference number to avoid later mix-ups. You may want to include the name of the writer, or use numbers to retain confidentiality.

Start by being receptive. Contemplate the page. Let the writing communicate with you. Turn the page around for a moment to get an overall impression of the general appearance of the handwriting. Record these first fresh impressions on your Check List.

It is only now that you start the active analysis, by considering in detail the three main components that make up the I.V.:

A. How does the general layout strike you?
Here you are considering the spacing or spatial distribution. The writing and the blank spaces around it should be balanced and in harmony. The script should be well proportioned. Consider the spacing of the margins, the spacing between the words and the lines and the paragraphs.

When you feel you have a definite impression, try to grade the general layout as above or below the middle line on the I.V. chart in the Check List. When you have established that, try to be more accurate. Did you judge the general layout 'above average' or 'superior'? Tick the appropriate square under 'A'. In practice, you will find that most writing falls broadly in the 'medium' category, subdivided into 'good' or 'fair'. The bottom square under 'A' represents 'below average' to 'inferior'.

B. Does the writing look natural?
Alternatively, does it look artificial? Or intended to impress by form (in the sense of style — ornate, for example, or designed)? Writing should be a method of expression, a means of communication. People usually write quickly and naturally, not intending to impress by form.

Consider whether you think the naturalness of the writing is above average to superior, a good or a fair average, or below average to inferior. When you have decided, tick one of the squares under 'B' in the I.V. chart.

C. Are the letter forms original?
Here you should ask yourself how far the letters resemble the letters the writer was taught to copy at school when learning to write. Adult writing that is still very similar to this 'copybook writing' is considered below average or fair, because it shows lack of development and individuality. A mature person should not communicate in the writing of an immature child. Adult writing should be mature and simplified – that is, leaving out unnecessary detail in the interests of speed, while retaining legibility (*see* p.62, samples 2 and 3). Compare, for example, the textbook letter 'g' on the left in the example below, with the equally readable example on the right, with its much more flowing movement and form.

Simplified letters can be compared with the work of modern painters, such as Matisse and Picasso, who simplified form, and increased originality and individual expression.

Consider whether the letter forms or ways of connecting them (*see* p.101) are conventional or original. When you have done so, tick one of the squares under 'C' in the I.V. chart.

I think with my ability to achieve targets working methods I know I can carry out any outstanding results.

Irregular script. Low average I.V. Lack of harmony.

In particular I'd like to know –
1) If the writing, and signatures, are by the same person?

Below average, inferior I.V.

Superior I.V.

of this election has
achievement for our
of the foundress

found very encouraging to you
feel deserve something for your

High I.V. script.

to our conversation
to enclose my C.V.

Regular script. Well
balanced. Not
overcontrolled. Good
medium I.V.

rights - and Treasury budgets - on the
revolts in 1990, only to see widespread
lowering the deaths of nearly twenty
last year or so, killed in ambushes
or in crashes of locally operated

Regular script.
Controlled. Fair
medium I.V.

lied to them in a partially prepared
task is to draw them roughly to shape,
in the manner required by the architect.
and the artistic temperament. of these
execution of any particular piece of

Positive and negative

The most important principle to remember is that
handwriting characteristics cannot be interpreted simplistically on the basis of one sign = one character trait. In
Chapter 1 we explained how the German graphologist
Ludwig Klages determined that any handwriting charac-

teristic can have a positive and a negative interpretation (*see* p.30). For example, large writing can be interpreted both as self-respect and as arrogance. How do you know which to use?

In most cases the I.V. values you noted in the I.V. chart in your Check List will give you a framework, or key, for your answers. If you categorized your sample as superior (above average) I.V., it will show more positive properties and fewer weaknesses; if you classified its I.V. as inferior (below average), it will have more negative interpretations. In the medium range I.V., positive and negative will co-exist fairly evenly.

If this seems hard to understand or put into practice, bear in mind the important discovery made back in the late 1880s (*see* p.27) that handwriting characteristics can be interpreted only in terms of their interrelationships. At this stage, therefore, all you can do is note the characteristics of the script you are studying and their possible interpretations, and wait until you have more results and can make more accurate judgements on the basis of more information.

Applying intrinsic value (I.V.)

Having determined the I.V. level, it is now useful to consider the significance of your findings. Here are some possible interpretations of I.V. for your analysis:

- An unexciting, dull person, leading a grey life, produces superficial, empty writing with little originality.
- Stylized writing is not created by warm inner life and depth. In fact it is a mask, a substitute for individual expression. Mannerism is a cover lacking perception and expression.

I.V. takes in regularity and rhythm. These attributes are part of our existence and of nature: the sun comes up and goes down, the seasons change. Animals move with rhythm; so do people. A script that gives an impression of harmony is rhythmic. The proportions are in harmony, the distances between the words are part of the total image, and there is balance between the black of the ink and the white of the paper. The words are spread evenly over the writing surface and the lines are clearly separated. Capitals are proportionate to the small letters.

The form and rhythm in handwriting tell you something

about the naturalness or the disturbance of a person's life. Wide spacing between words in one place and cramped spacing elsewhere creates unrhythmical writing, a sign of imbalance.

Disturbances in rhythm point to unresolved conflicts between the conscious and the unconscious, with its drives, repressed needs and longings. You can see this in the preponderance of unrhythmic writing among mentally ill people and drug addicts (*see* p.115).

In addition to experience, you need feeling and intuition to determine the I.V. at a glance. (Jung defines intuition as 'perception via the unconscious'.) However, to be objective in your interpretation, you should always follow these guidelines:

- Too much of any aspect is detrimental to the I.V.: too small a script or too large, too extended, too regular or irregular, too wide or too narrow.
- Rapid writing indicates initiative and industriousness, but remember that a person who speaks too quickly shows turmoil and agitation, and becomes incoherent.
- Superior or high I.V. writing points to creativity, but too much creativity may take us into the land of daydreams, fantasy or playing to the gallery.

When you have decided on a possible interpretation of your findings, record it on your Check List in preparation for your final analysis and report.

The spatial dimension

The next stage is to analyse these impressions in greater detail. You should still refrain from reading your sample or studying the writing too closely: you must begin by considering the spaces between and around the writing.

One's first impressions of a letter or sheet of writing are largely gained from what is called the spatial proportioning — the balance between writing and space on the page, which you considered when establishing the I.V. of your sample. This balance contributes to the aesthetic impression a letter or sheet of writing makes.

The components of spatial proportioning can be broken down into margins, the spacing between paragraphs, the spacing between the lines, the word-spacing and the letter-spacing. We will consider each one in turn.

Margins

Your first impression of the use of space on a page comes from the margins. The distribution of black and white on the page — in other words, the positioning of the margins around the writing and their size — are what make a page look balanced. On your Check List is a representation of a page on which you should record the appearance of the margins in your sample, in the same way as the examples given on p.66—7. Look carefully at each of the margins in turn, and note on the Check List whether and where it is wide or narrow, straight or wavy. Follow the line with your pencil. Measure its width in various places and add the measurements to the Check List, noting whether the margins veer to the left or the right.

The breadth of the margins, especially the left margin, indicates the distance the writer wishes to maintain from the outside world. Margins are strong indicators of the left-right symbolism that applies to many handwriting features (*see* p.57). Wide left margins are typical of reserved or proud people; wide right margins are typical of extreme self-consciousness. Wide margins all round indicate withdrawal — or a highly developed aesthetic sense.

A writer who leaves no margins may be indicating a need for constant close contact with others; alternatively he or she may be prying, greedy or intrusive — or generous, kind, very interested in other people. A person who leaves no left-hand margin is likely to be fearful of the future.

The distribution of margins also gives a clue to the writer's planning ability — clearly, the writer who runs short of space at the end of each sentence, or at the end of the letter, fails to plan.

As they write, most writers lose consciousness of their margins, perhaps moving gradually rightward, indicating impatience perhaps or enthusiasm or a desire to establish closer bonds with the person to whom they are writing. Writers whose left margin narrows may be shy, prudent or extremely reserved. Symbolism is obviously pertinent here.

Here is a summary of the possible positive and negative interpretations of the margins in a handwriting sample. Read through them and note the most likely interpretations of your own samples on your Check List.

Margin and line variations.

	POSITIVE	NEGATIVE

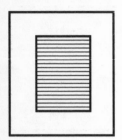

Margins all round

sense of proportion	childish, undeveloped
feeling for design	restricted spontaneity
detached	defensive attitude
aesthetic	formalistic, posing

Increasing left margin

spontaneous	impressionable
lively	impatient
extravert	
expressive	
committed	

Decreasing left margin

introverted	withdrawn
prudent	afraid to be spontaneous
acts after consideration	suspicious

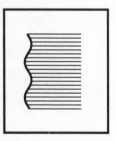

Zig-zag left margin

open to stimuli, receptive   unstable, erratic, moody

    alternately spontaneous and prudent
    alternately introverted and extrovert
    has conflicting impulses to give and urges to retain
    over-hasty *or* indecisive

POSITIVE	NEGATIVE

Constant left margin

disciplined	childish, undeveloped
stable	not spontaneous, rigid

Broad right margin

prudent	tends to hold back
aesthetic	fearful of life's hard edges
distant	experiences a remoteness between the Self and the Other
	fearful of the future
	fearful of binding decisions

No right margin

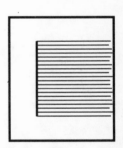

decision-maker	lacks tact
uninhibited	incautious, unguarded
	lacks overview
	over-eager

Straight right margin

self-disciplined	lacks spontaneity

Spacing

The page is the symbolic stage on which the writer performs the act of writing. The way writers use the page before them — the blank writing space — mirrors their relationship to the outside world. Every distance in the writing is a distance to the Other: the outer world.

A pleasing distance between lines is such that they are wide enough apart to be clearly distinguishable as lines and that the upper and lower extensions of the letters do not run into each other — or 'mingle'. A pleasing distance between words is a space the size of a letter 'm' or 'n'.

Note the distances between lines and words in your sample and record them on your Check List.

When the space is used well, words and lines are clearly separated, indicating clarity of thought, organizing ability and a balanced perspective. If the base line of the writing is straight, the writer shows goal-directedness.

In word-spacing we project the relationship between the I and the Other: the outside world. The unconscious way in which the word-spacing comes about makes it psychologically more important than the line-spacing. A skilled writer will continue the writing movement uninterrupted from the beginning to the end of the line. A new line requires an interruption and a reorientation. With large gaps, the directness is lost. Large word–distance writers can feel quite lonely.

In women this is often caused by the lack of a secure and warm tie with the father in early youth, resulting in later life in feelings of loneliness and isolation. Everyone's personality develops at least partly in response to example. For the girl growing up, the father figure is a unifying and protecting umbrella, a shield that should eventually fade away or become superfluous. As she grows up, her psyche ripens, and she can detach herself from him and reach out to others. Such a fluent development fosters a spontaneous personality with easy social skills, close to others where appropriate in new and business contacts.

The story reverses if the father died or the parents divorced or if the father was a bully or weak, not inspiring trust in the girl. Without father-bonding, psychic inhibitions rise, and this shows up in large distances between words.

Such people are anxious to give themselves, yet afraid of being disappointed again. Because they lack the right father-figure, they learn at an early age that they must take the initiative or nothing happens. Although they are not adult in their feelings, they begin to organize and to take charge of things themselves. Deep down they feel insecure, but in whatever they do they give a very independent impression. They oscillate between dependence and independence, both longing for and fearing deep relationships.

Lack of father–bonding is difficult to overcome, even for women with abundant beauty, intelligence and talent. The psychological inhibitions feed a cerebral approach, and this can result in endless analysis of people and events, which is in fact based on lack of confidence.

With an understanding boss, or when working independently, as a colleague in a female team, such women can be excellent in their work. However, if they feel let down, their reaction may be vehement and the working relationship may well be damaged beyond repair. Fortunately, mothers are an equally or even more important factor in the formation of the personality, often at least partly compensating for the shortcomings of the father. Nature is a great balancer.

In men, good mother–bonding is of great importance for a close and warm relationship with the opposite sex, and in marriage. The backing of a solid, supportive, loving partner and family life is of immense value, even for the most self-confident man, especially in times of trouble in business. When the relationship between father and mother causes problems, the young man may become reserved or refuse to take sides. If the father was inadequate or overbearing and the bond with his mother was good, the young man may find his own way quite well, but if his bond with his mother was weak he may never escape his father's shadow.

The basis for self-confidence in later life is acquired in early childhood, and is of paramount importance for both sexes.

Wide word-spacing with normal distance between the lines indicates correct demeanour and behaviour in public situations, together with a reserved attitude towards others.

Uneven distances between words indicates oscillation between spontaneity and inhibition; alternating approach and distancing oneself from people. Such people may therefore be socially erratic — friendly one minute and aloof the next. They may also be slow decision-makers in business.

Narrow word-spacing indicates a great need for contact and, if the writing is wide as well, spontaneity.

If the word-spacing is narrow and the lines mingle (the descenders run into the upper loops of the line below) the writer may well be pushy and lack tact. Mingling of lines in a high I.V. writing can indicate an abundance of imagination.

Narrow line-*spacing.*
'Mingling',
overlapping. Narrow
word-spacing.

Hong Kong. It will be our last day out there. Next is Bangkok and we intend to stay there at least a week before we fly to Indonesia. First stop will be Bali.

Good distribution
of black and white.
Line-spacing clear.
Word-spacing
balanced.

Hong Kong. It will be our last day out there. Next is Bangkok and we intend to stay there at least a week before we fly to Indonesia First stop will be Bali.

Clear, but large
spaces between words.

Hong Kong. It will be our last day out there. Next is Bangkok and we intend to stay there at least a week

In low I.V. writing, mingling denotes lack of clarity — even confusion — and lack of objectivity.

The old French school of graphology used to teach that mingling lines invariably indicates confusion in thinking. Robert Saudek, the Austrian-born graphologist who researched criteria for discovering dishonesty in writing, demonstrated that the opposite can be the case — when, for example, abstract thinking is directed at problems outside the practical sphere, creating a world in itself.

Beethoven is a prime example of this. Alfred Mendel, author of the American classic *Personality in Handwriting* (1946) called his writing 'a battlefield hand' and wrote that 'his stirring compositions were conceived out of chaos'. Genius is not concerned with clear formulation for easy understanding by the layperson. Some minglers lose contact with their contemporaries. They are simply light years ahead, creating a new world, tomorrow's world or a new universe.

Beethoven's handwriting.

On the ink trail

Line direction

Study your sample carefully and note on the Check List whether the lines are straight, rising, falling, concave and so on.

Rising or falling 'tiles' is a succession of words that rise or fall from the base line.

Falling tiles.

Line direction is less constant than other script characteristics because it is dependent on mood, as well as will. For accurate analysis it is best to have examples of writing characteristics produced over a period of time. As with all writing characteristics, more than one explanation is possible and the conclusion must be based on a number of indications in the script. For example, straight lines can originate from self-discipline, even temper and balance, or from lack of vitality, emotion or originality.

Line direction (place a transparent ruler under the line of writing).

Straight, horizontal
lines.

Rising lines.

Falling (descending)
lines.

Rising tiles.

Falling (descending)
tiles.

Convex lines.

Concave lines.

Wavering lines.

Below are lists of the positive and negative symbolism associated with line direction. Note the symbolism you consider most appropriate to your handwriting sample in your Check List.

POSITIVE	NEGATIVE

Straight, horizontal lines

balanced	unlively
goal-orientated	unadventurous, dull
sticks to own plans	rigid, unbending
disciplined	unoriginal

Rising lines

strong need for self- expression	unrestrained tense, strained
optimistic	restless
has an appetite for work	
creative	
enthusiastic	

Falling lines

if falling slightly:
   resists depression
   tries to cope with
   burden of work
	discouraged
	depressive
	lacklustre frame of mind
	pessimistic
	overworked

Rising tiles

strong urge to express feelings
   but makes an effort to keep control
resists own aggressive tendencies
   with varying success

Descending tiles

strongly resists sombre, depressive thoughts

Convex lines

enthusiastic start is tailing off due to lack
   of energy and perseverance
flash-in-the-pan temperament

Concave lines

---

starts reluctantly, gradually warms up
and perseveres

Wavering lines

---

lack of inner security
easily influenced
subject to mood changes
unstable
changes mind and goal
posts

*Wavy line starting and
finishing at the same height*

---

capacity to make use of
opportunities and reach ultimate goals

Horizontal tension

This is the degree to which a word or a series of words adhere to the base line. Surprise yourself by applying a straight, transparent rule along the base of each word in what seems a taut, straight line of writing. You may well find that it is in fact convex, concave or wavy.

A relaxed horizontal tension (HT) in a script is always straight and hardly varying in its flow towards the right-hand margin of the page. HT merits a positive interpretation when it is accompanied by light to medium pressure and every letter is associated with rightward tendencies (RT). Weak pressure with vertical slant may not indicate lack of purpose, but more control is required to achieve the end result. Check with other factors, such as regularity and rhythm, and note where breaks occur — that is, where irregularities occur in a regular script, where the rhythm changes and so on.

HT that is too taut indicates difficulty in reaching out, especially if accompanied by leftward tendencies (LT). If associated with heavy writing pressure (*see* p.88), tension may be suspected.

Weak HT means a difficulty in maintaining goals in life. The desire to sustain an effort may not be realized.

POSITIVE	NEGATIVE

Taut horizontal tension

steadiness	holds back
level-headedness	fear
persistence	lack of ease
ability to complete tasks	rigidity
drive and tenacity	compulsive perfectionism

Rhythm

Writing is regular when the small middle zone (MZ) letters (*see* p.56) are about the same size, when the downstrokes run about parallel, the distances between the downstrokes are about equal and the lines are straight. You will need to study your sample carefully to be able to grade its rhythm on the Check List as good, fair, irregular or rigid.

Everyone has an individual, unique rhythm. Only a machine can produce absolute regularity. The more our activities allow us to fall in with our internal rhythm, the happier and more effective we will be in our work and leisure. Air travellers need to give their inner clocks time to adjust to a new time zone and recover from jet-lag. Women need

Regular   Rigid   Irregular

to take their monthly biological time clocks into consideration in their working lives, to avoid creating stress.

To achieve anything you need a certain self-discipline and perseverance. Regular writing with strong pressure indicates a character capable of overcoming resistance and difficulties. People with regular writing stick to the same direction and concentrate their powers, which requires effort. Impulsive inclinations are kept in check and the energy is goal-directed.

However, this positive interpretation of rhythmic writing is valid only if a strong emotional inner life is channelled by an even stronger will. If the regularity is monotonous and rigid, the writer may be insensitive, a stereotype, lacking in warmth. Rigid regularity points to strong emotional repression.

Mood versus mind.
Irregular writing.

An unbalanced person writes irregularly: the downstrokes

I am now casting about for the right thing to do and hope that your analysis might be one factor that help to steer me in the right direction.

Regular writing as taught in the 1930s.

the beaches which were mostly very clean and sandy. The weather too, was very benign, sunny and warm with only 1 day having a mist in from the sea.

Irregular writing.
Lack of will-power.

I think that my principal weakness is communication.

Rigid regularity. Full of will-power. Tense.

I was very pleased to meet you last week to Company and the extensive product range. my experience and potential of interest.

vary in direction, the sizes of the letters vary and the lines undulate. The accent is on feeling and emotion, but also on spontaneity. An irregular writer is able to express his or her psychic life with minimal inhibition and easily establishes contact with others. If there are signs of originality and richness of ideas in an irregular writing with a good I.V., there is also creativity.

If irregular writing is too weak, however, there is failing will, instability and often insecurity. If the downstrokes are slanting left, right and centre, there is lack of self-discipline and strong inner contradictions. These are indications of immaturity — puberty retained — even at an advanced age.

Writers with regular script are in general better suited to routine tasks than irregular writers. The latter have a more restless inner life, and more need for variety and diversity.

POSITIVE	NEGATIVE
Regular writing	
harmonious	lacks feeling
balanced	rigid
constant	unmovable
disciplined	hard
firm	colourless
determined	stereotypical
vital	cool
strong-willed	
persevering	
stamina	
Irregular writing	
sensitive	weak-willed
temperamental	unstable
spontaneous	rudderless
able to adjust to	unsure
circumstances	easily influenced
original	unpredictable
creative	

Vanity

The three zones: upper, middle and lower zone (UZ, MZ, LZ)

The symbolism of the three zones (*see* p.56) was not dreamed up in modern times by psychologists who practise graphology. Long ago the human personality was considered to consist of three aspects: the head (spirit), the soul (the senses and the heart), and the body (the lower part containing the vital and sexual functions).

Plato placed the intelligence in the head, the spirit in the chest and desire in the lower part of the body. We are used to imagining the intelligence or spirit, soul and body in a top-to-bottom arrangement. This trichotomy, assimilated and refined by modern psychology, becomes a point of departure for our observation and analysis of handwriting.

A strong predominance of the upper zone (UZ), upper loops and other upper extensions from the middle zone (MZ) indicates a strong spiritual interest and idealism, which, if the lower zone (LZ) is underdeveloped, can indicate lack of realism. In such a writer, ideas lose their relation to reality and enter the domain of fantasy. The writing is like a tree without solid roots, easily toppled.

Upper Zone
Middle Zone
Lower Zone

Accent on the LZ indicates a greater sense of reality. The dominant interests are pulling towards the physical, the sexual and the material side of life. This could result in materialism and lack of idealism — but bear in mind that you must not reach such a conclusion before ensuring that other indications in the script confirm your impression. Large underloops can indicate a strong sexuality, but also vanity.

Dominant lower extensions.

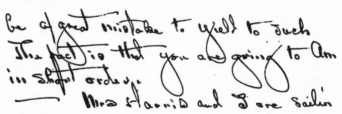

The handwriting of Paul P. Harris, President Emeritus, Rotary International, reproduced with kind permission of the magazine *Rotary*, Aug/Sept. 1991.

Generally speaking, if UZ loops are a dominant feature in a high I.V. writing, there is warmth of feeling and good harmony with the unconscious, provided that the loops are connected with the following letter. Dominant UZ loops in a lower I.V. writing can indicate rigidity and coldness. Long UZ loops, good I.V. and strong pressure indicate resilience and vitality.

Accent on the middle zone (MZ) signifies preoccupation with day-to-day events and daily existence. If upper and lower extensions are too small by comparison, there is too little spiritual interest and too little contact with the deeper layers of the personality. Good proportions between the zones in a higher-level I.V. script show a balanced personality. Lower-level I.V. and slow writing indicate inertia.

Balance

POSITIVE   NEGATIVE

Dominant upper extensions

idealistic	superficial
interest in the spiritual	impractical
enthusiastic	easily carried away
strives for deeper insight	lack of common sense
	fear of the sexual

Dominant lower extensions

stable, down-to-earth	lack of idealism
realistic, materialistic	not easily moved
strong gut feelings	mentally inert
healthy sexual life	urges rule intellect

DIFFERENCES IN LENGTH

By this we mean the proportion between long UZ and LZ letters, and the MZ letters (those of 'a', 'c', 'e' height). Extending upper and lower loops and other extensions indicate, with good I.V., dynamism, vitality, progression and liveliness, but also inner unrest. Pride stimulates the urge for achievement.

With lower I.V., we detect inner dissatisfaction, and discrepancy between willingness and ability.

With good level I.V. and equally proportioned upper and lower lengths in relation to the MZ, we observe inner balance and maturity, an equilibrium between mind and instinct. Pulver points out that maturity tempers excess.

POSITIVE	NEGATIVE

Large differences in length

POSITIVE	NEGATIVE
dynamic	discrepancy between
enterprising	willingness and ability
showing initiative	immature
lively	dissatisfied
progressive	unbalanced
	egocentric

Small differences in length

POSITIVE	NEGATIVE
mature	lacking interest
satisfied	limited
balanced	inert
modest	

Rightward and leftward tendencies

This does not describe the political leanings of the writer — tendencies towards the left or the right indicate, respectively, tendencies towards introversion (LT) or extraversion (RT). Such tendencies are not only expressed in the slant of the handwriting but also in the habit of the writer to veer in the opposite direction from the logical one — a left movement where right movements are called for, and vice versa. The term describes, for example, the direction in which an 'o' is written or the direction of the ascender on a 'd'.

Rightward movement: 'g' and 'y' move to the right, 't' bars and 'i' dots rightwards from the stem. Outward directedness.

Leftward movement: 'd', 'i' dot, 't' bar move leftwards from the stem. Inward directedness.

RT writing shows the need for contact and the ability to move away from one's own patch — to reach out. The writer of a high I.V. script with RT will be altruistic and uninhibited, but an RT writer with a low I.V. script will exhibit submission and lack of will-power.

LT script indicates an urge to self-preservation and self-centredness. The egocentric personality is inclined toward self-concern and withdrawal, yet it seems that self-preservation and personal development are best served by less concentration on the self and greater directedness toward other people, or by activity. Action leads to greater psychic satisfaction. Lurking behind egocentricity may well be a deep-seated fear of the Other. Those too busy with their own Self remain shuttered, inhibiting the opening-up of the psyche and preventing it from flourishing. Typical signs of *A defensive attitude* the hemmed-in personality are the rolled 'a', 'd' and 'o' in an LT script.

dare to

POSITIVE	NEGATIVE
RT writing	
altruistic	difficulty in saying no
adaptable	easily carried away
extravert	flies from Self into
affable	adventure
sympathetic	dependent
expansive	weak-willed
goal-directed	restless
LT writing	
independent	egotistical
contemplative	self-centred
steadfast	greedy, acquisitive
resolute	lacking compassion
	uncompromising

Submissive

First and final letters

INITIAL STROKES AND LETTERS

If you think of the paper on which you write as the stage and the writer as an actor, the first letter of a word can be compared with the actor's entrance. It could be full of confidence and with natural gusto or unsure and shy. Writers who embellish initial letters, widen or enlarge them or pen them with stronger pressure than the rest of the word they introduce, accentuate themselves; they pay considerable attention to their demeanour and the impression they make on others. In extreme cases these features indicate arrogance and inordinate assertiveness.

Bear in mind, however, that such characteristics should not be interpreted on their own, but should be compared with other handwriting features and be seen in the light of the I.V. As you will see in Chapter 4, one sign does not warrant definite conclusions and can be misleading.

Healthy confidence is indicated by natural writing, in which the size, width and pressure of the capitals are kept in proportion to the following letters in a word.

Initial letters that are narrower than the rest of the word indicate a measure of shyness and self-consciousness at the start. Spontaneity awakens if the following letters widen up.

Hey, you!

If the second downstroke of the capital letter 'H' towers high above the first, the writer is highly assertive. The person showing this characteristic is capable of great effort, dedication and application. He or she will always respond to a word of appreciation.

Hey, you!

If, on the other hand, the capital letter is narrow, the writer is more vulnerable than is apparent and is disappointed, suffering from injured pride or feeling unappreciated.

Hey, you!

Capitals starting with a dot indicate an inhibited personality. Making contacts does not come easily.

Capitals with flourishes point to egocentricity.

A straight starting stroke anchored far under the MZ line indicates a pugnacious writer given to aggressive reactions and possibly also intolerant and unreasonable.

Anchored

A powerful script shows a commitment to industriousness: the writer 'likes to get on with it'. Strength of script is indicated by pressure on the paper.

Curved starting strokes anchored far under the MZ line point to long-windedness.

Anchored

A fast script without starting strokes shows that the writer quickly gains familiarity with the task in hand, and makes contact easily.

FINAL STROKES AND LETTERS

The last letter of a word, a sentence or a paragraph is symbolic of an actor's exit, so let us now look at the way the writer leaves the stage.

If the beginning of a word is similar in appearance to the end, the writer behaves naturally.

Diminishing word-endings in a good I.V. script denote empathy. Increasing size toward the end can indicate naïvety, but also pushiness.

Increased pressure in the endstrokes indicates a lively temperament. People who write like this emphasize their opinions and find it difficult to cope with objections.

Unfinished final strokes show caution and a tendency not to reveal too much about oneself.

Unfinished downstrokes ending above the writing line — so-called 'hanging script' — indicate strong inhibitions.

Size

THE LARGE SCRIPT

When measuring the size of a script, you take the letters of the middle zone (MZ; *see* p.56) as the median.

Large is larger than 3mm. Small is smaller than 2mm. Medium is between the two.

Someone whose writing is large requires space, and likes action and results. A large writing movement shows an urge for expansion and a sense of self-esteem. A large script with a good I.V. and with strong pressure (*see below*) radiates power and the qualities of leadership, coupled with self-respect, concerned and independent behaviour.

A large script with a lower I.V. indicates arrogant, presumptuous behaviour (*see below*). Large writing is often an over-compensation for an original inferiority complex. The stronger this inferiority complex, the stronger the assertiveness. Drive, ambition and aggression co-exist. The writer of a large script thinks on the larger scale, rather than tending to concentrate on details, and wants power and achievement.

Large garland-type writing (*see* p.101) with a high I.V. level points to warmth of feeling and originality. If the writing is large, wide and speedy, the writer has a strongly outward-directed character, but a tendency to dissoluteness.

Arrogance

THE SMALL SCRIPT

The writer of a small script is characterized by more modesty and realism, and is more critical and objective. A low I.V. coupled with a small script indicates insecurity, short-sightedness and lack of enthusiasm.

A writer whose script is rhythmic, but varies in size, is lively and impressionable. An unrhythmic writer is moody and restless — forces from the subconscious upset the balance.

In high I.V. writing, steadiness, self-control and inner security are expressed in small, evenly sized MZ letters.

POSITIVE	NEGATIVE

Large writing

self-respecting	arrogant
takes a wide view	given to pipe-dreaming
enterprising	superficial
outspoken	exaggerated
big-hearted	conceited
enthusiastic	uninhibited
persuasive	exalted
willing to take risks	unrealistic

Small writing

modest	has inferiority complex
realistic	unimaginative
businesslike	dry
deliberate	narrow-minded
attends to detail	niggling
able to concentrate	has narrow horizons

Width

THE WIDE SCRIPT

A script is wide in the graphological sense if the distances between the downstrokes of the letters 'm' and 'n' are larger than their height, provided the upstrokes and downstrokes separate.

In narrow writing, the height of the downstrokes is more than the distance between them.

Width expresses spontaneity, symbolic giant strides toward the Other, the goal, the future. Instead of concentration on the Self, there is a strong, spontaneous push towards the external. Those who believe in the future are optimistic and head straight for it, with an eager eye open for opportunities.

A script that is wide but irregular shows signs of too little self-discipline; the writer may tend toward profligacy and superficiality.

Wide writers with high I.V. mix easily, are not afraid to follow their feelings and are interested in self-development. However, their pliant outlook may also indicate extravagance and a tendency to go over the top. Width in writing can also originate from a flight away from loneliness and Self, creating risk and adventure, with some danger.

Wide script with a left slant shows prudence or conflict between spontaneity and prudence – the car driver accelerating one moment and slamming on the brakes a moment later. In general, the wide writer is more adaptable than the narrow writer, more extrovert than introvert.

POSITIVE	NEGATIVE
Wide writing	
extrovert	profligate
spontaneous	unrestrained
open	impetuous
goal-directed	casual
active	tends to flee into work or
good mixer	adventure
industrious	extravagant
	restless
Narrow writing	
disciplined	rigid
detached	inhibited
considered	doubting
deliberate	defensive
prudent	shy
	not spontaneous
	untrusting
	calculating
	does not mix easily

THE NARROW SCRIPT

Narrowness is connected with keeping to oneself, reserve, feelings kept in check. The positive side of the narrow writer emphasizes contemplation and composure, but there is often also angst, and a vague, inner restraint. At the slightest provocation the shutters are brought down to keep the cool in.

Narrow writers are difficult to fathom, wary of risk, shunning new projects; they are more static than dynamic. They often fear the future, lack trust and confidence, and have an urge to protect themselves, even when self-protection is uncalled for. Some ooze tension and heaviness of heart, strongly reflecting anxiety and inhibition.

Narrow writing often originates in childhood, when strong discipline and domestic tyranny or some other repression strangled spontaneity and openness, making seclusion and inner isolation the least risky tactic. If parents are spontaneous, if children are more encouraged than held back, they will not develop these characteristics, and will make the transition from adolescence to maturity more easily. They will be less likely to be shy and will find it easier to make contacts than those pushed into inner isolation.

Scrooges have narrow handwriting. An 'o' can be so narrow that up and downstrokes overlap. This is a sign of prudence and slight inhibition — or, as Dr Max Pulver claimed, insincerity.

Narrowness in the first letters alone shows initial hesitation by the writer. Alternating width and narrowness in the script indicates on and off spontaneity and holding back.

Stroke quality

It is the ink trail a writer leaves that forms the letters and the connections between them. The appearance of the ink trail depends to a great extent on the writer's choice of nib — thick, thin, broad, fine, hard or soft — and the way the pen is held.

Some people select their pen almost as if it were a weapon to be used on a battlefield — the paper. A firm pen will dig trenches in the paper and will not buckle under strong pressure. Broad nibs suggest warmth, comfort, sensuality. Fine nibs indicate refinement, fragility and coldness.

The pen you choose and the way you hold it are reflections of your personality. Holding the pen close to the nib indicates precision, goal-directedness, discipline and rationality. A more relaxed and less close grip, resulting in a more horizontal position of the pen, increases the point of contact, makes the stroke spread slightly — a phenomenon known as 'pastosity' (*see* p.110) — and is identified with gut-feeling before reason, sensuality, spontaneity, lack of inhibition and a happy, earthy disposition, though sometimes bordering on carelessness and even neglect. Stroke quality is also affected by writing pressure.

Writing pressure

Strong pressure via the pen to the writing surface will show up in heavy or split strokes if a fountain pen is used or a welt at the back of the paper if a ballpoint is used. With other writing implements, conclusions about pressure will have to be drawn from the shape and continuity of the lettering and connections. Slight pressure will show fine lines.

Pressure indicates available energy. Rhythmic pressure accentuates the downstrokes; this is followed by a release in the upstrokes. Strong, rhythmic pressure in a writing with a high I.V. indicates powerful energy, vitality, will-power and stamina, provided the writing is not too irregular. Strong pressure with rigidity — like goose-stepping soldiers — shows up a writer with inhibitions, with an inclination towards harshness and obstinacy.

POSITIVE	NEGATIVE

Strong pressure

strong–willed	rigid
stable	hard
male	aggressive
decisive	brooding
energetic	insensitive
has a strong driving force	opinionated
firm	cheeky
resistant	fierce
has fighting spirit	

Little pressure

adaptable	a pushover
female	dependent
perceptive	limp
compliant	weak–willed
adroit	unstable
prudent	anxious

Order verses chaos

Irregular writing with strong pressure is a manifestation of inner disturbance, defiance, vehemence, and a hidden yearning for friction and argument. Inner tension can cause increased pressure or originate from strained effort.

Increased pressure is a typical male feature; decreased pressure more characteristic of the writing of women. People who write with little pressure are more accommodating, flexible, sensitive and adaptable, but do not expect a forceful personality with abundant energy. Little pressure in irregular script points to lack of will-power, but more empathy and mental agility than the writer with heavy pressure. Light pressure can also result from physical weakness.

If the increased pressure does not appear in the downstrokes, but suddenly here and there, expect the writer to discharge inner tensions aggressively and suddenly.

Increased pressure in capitals only wants to impress. Side pressure — on a horizontal stroke, such as a 't' bar, is frequently reported in the writing of technicians. It is, however, also often found in cases of neurosis and nervous disorder.

Handwriting slant

Slant is the angle of the writing measured from the horizontal base line of the script. Handwriting can slant rightward from

the vertical, be upright at approximately 90 degrees or slant leftward. Allow for some variation of slant in your handwriting sample. The way handwriting slants symbolizes the way in which the writer's contact with the outer world comes about.

Handwriting slant. 'Too much' spells problems. Take a pencil to elongate the slant of several letters up and downwards to facilitate measuring the angle.

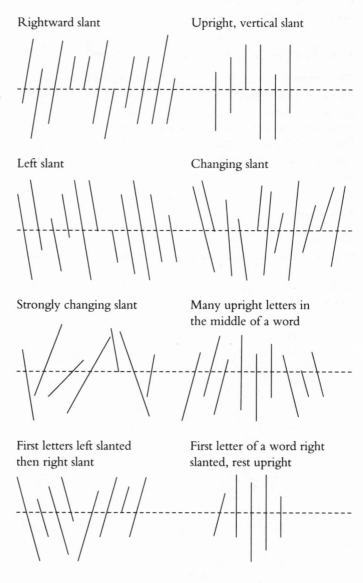

Rightward slant

Upright, vertical slant

Left slant

Changing slant

Strongly changing slant

Many upright letters in the middle of a word

First letters left slanted then right slant

First letter of a word right slanted, rest upright

Right slant

Rightward-slanting letters are moving ahead to the environment, seeking contact with the Other. The writer reacts spontaneously; seeks friendship and company. If the slant is too far to the right, towards the horizontal, the writer is too impressionable, likely to be susceptible to impulses from both within and without, and in danger of losing control and independence.

Upright script or vertical slant

The letters stand up: the mind takes charge over impulses; reserve reigns. 'Think before you act' is the motto. Stiff upper lip is the stance towards life. Independence and aloofness could lead to calculation and lack of feeling for others. During adolescence writing slant can vary, becoming more upright, reflecting introspection and sometimes fear of increasing physical urges.

Left slant

This indicates holding off, bending back, showing passive resistance and inner reserve. It can be the result of a traumatic experience, a barricade erected. The first reaction is 'no' or 'wait a minute'. In personal contacts, actions may well be the reverse of the expected. For some, protest becomes a way of life.

Many young women with left-slanted handwriting feel attracted to older men, as a protection against life's hard edges. Women with left-slanted handwriting tend to initiate relationships — by flirting, for example, but not meaning it — and thus trying to take control. If they win, they may give the impression that they are more spontaneous and involved in the situation than they really are. In fact, they take a long time to warm towards anyone. Once they form a bond, however, the chances are that it will be solid and long-lasting. Women of this type often make very good secretaries. Their posture is merely a defence against inner insecurity.

Ludwig Klages (*see* p.30) believed that left slant indicates self-conquest. There is considerable doubt among graphologists about this opinion.

Wide slant differences, irregularity, wide spaces between words – this first sample of writing indicated deep-seated problems.

> I would like to become more computer literate over the next year and with this in mind I am reading and attending courses about computers. It has been suggested that I purchase a computer, which will help me

Two years later the writer had started to tackle these, with dramatic results for and through his writing (see second sample). The final problem to be tackled was legibility, improvement in communications. This meant, in writing, back to basics, almost copybook style.

> provided a base to build my confidence. I feel I am much more positive than I have been for a long time, as I contemplate. my future.

POSITIVE	NEGATIVE
Rightward slant	
extravert	reckless
needs contact	can be carried away
cordial, warm	lacks independence
sociable	not detached enough
adaptable	uncontrolled
willing to have a go	
spontaneous	
committed	
Upright script	
rational	cool
independent	unsociable
self-conscious	finds it hard to adapt to
disciplined	situations
thinks before acting	tends to pose
level-headed	calculating

Leftward slant

inhibited
instinctively keeps a distance
inwardly holds off
harbours an adolescent . or immature attitude of defiance
difficult to approach

Changing slant

contradictory feelings and inner struggle

Strongly changing slant

unbalanced personality, unstable, unharmonious

Many upright letters in the middle of a word

varying mind control or impulses

First letters left-slanted, remainder right-slanted

initial reserve overcome by
spontaneity

First letter of a word right-slanted, the rest upright

after first impulse, prudence reigns (Pulver)

The 'i' dots and 't' bars

Too much has been written about these. Diacritics, dots, bars and accent marks in other languages are essential parts of letters, and so of interest, but they should not be interpreted without reference to other features in the script.

If the 'i' dots and 't' bars are placed with precision, it is an indication of accuracy. Forgetfulness and lack of concentration are indicated if they are left out. A dot towards the right of the 'i' indicates speed and a critical mind. Dots to the left are found in the writing of prudent, often inhibited people who lack self-confidence.

In a high I.V. writing 'i' dots and 't' bars connected with the letters following them indicate above-average intelligence, powers of combination and deduction, speedy reasoning and acuteness. Such connections are often found in the script of psychoanalysts, writers, artists and policy makers.

We are often asked the meaning of a small circle instead of an 'i' dot. It obviously indicates slow writing speed, but artists, designers and architects often use it in their desire to be different. In the writing of teenagers it indicates a need for attention.

Resting dots

The price of disciplined virtuosity working under pressure is stress. The example below was written by a graphic artist working in Northern Ireland. His stress level is visualized by the frequency of resting dots in his writing.

Grapho-speed

Speed in handwriting is not as simple as so many letters or words per minute, like typing speed or shorthand speed. Dr Robert Saudek, a well known graphologist who practised in London in the 1930s, first studied the rate at which different people write, using film recording and measurement, and the results of his research, together with the findings of others who followed him, have been widely adopted. Rather than time people writing, handwriting analysts look for signs in their script that indicate fast or slow writing, signs which are symbolic of personality traits. We prefer to use the term 'grapho-speed' to describe speed in handwriting. This term encompasses the features that signify quickness or slowness in handwriting and their symbolic meaning.

We have found combinations of the features listed below significant. When there are more characteristics of speed than slowness, the writing is fast; otherwise it is slow.

Signs of fast writing

1. Smooth, unbroken strokes with rhythmically changing pressure — less pressure on the upstrokes, more on the downstrokes.
2. Immediacy of the writing movement — no starting strokes, for example.
3. Uncertainty of aim in diacritic signs: 'i' dots and 't' bars are jotted down to the right of the main body of the letter.
4. Much rightward directional tendency and a widening left-hand margin.
5. Little interruption in the writing — whole words are written in one go. Diacritics are connected to the letters or dots following them and there are more round than angular forms.
6. Curtailed and degenerated letters towards the ends of words.
7. Large spaces between the downstrokes of a single letter, and between separate letters.
8. Ascending lines (as long as the paper is in a normal position).

Signs of slow writing

1. Wavering forms and broken strokes with little or suddenly occurring pressure.
2. Conspicuous certainty of aim, with 'i' dots and 't' bars almost exactly above or near the main body of the letter.
3. Decreasing left margin and frequent leftward directional tendencies.
4. Frequent writing pauses; dots, blobs in letters. More disconnected letters and angular forms and connections.
5. Precise execution of letter forms; ornamentation.
6. Narrow letters with little space between downstrokes and letter forms, possibly causing covering strokes.
7. Descending lines.

Fast writers are direct, spontaneous, lively and agile; they like to exchange ideas. They think and work quickly. Their attitude is typically informal and straightforward. In a script with a good I.V., speed indicates self-confidence and natural behaviour. Quick writers feel at home and at ease anywhere, and are generally cheerful and enterprising. However, they need variety. On the negative side they lack restraint, and tend to be agitated and restless.

Slow writing indicates greater prudence – but greater inhibition. Slow writers prefer to be on the safe side. Their positive qualities are level-headedness, calm and steadiness. Negative traits include slowness, indecision and lack of self-confidence.

Excessive speed and slowness are both considered negative indications: going over the top on the one hand or down the drain on the other. Writing that is too fast can deteriorate into chaos and total illegibility. Extreme speed may mean disorganized, chaotic, hysterical or even psychotic behaviour. However, it can also signify boredom with routine (as in doctors' writing).

Writing that is too slow may be legible, but will often be static and laboured. Extreme slowness often indicates poor intelligence and illiteracy. Dishonesty is also associated with very slow speed – but only in combination with several other factors (*see* p.117).

Strong personalities translate thought into action, which conquers doubt. Weak personalities find it difficult to be spontaneous and to express feelings and thoughts. They often hold up a bogus façade, a mask, an inflated persona – a pseudo personality – for external consumption. This, however, has to be upheld. In reality it has at its root disabling and self-fulfilling inferiority complexes and impotence.

Masking, the persona

POSITIVE	NEGATIVE
Fast writing	
active	inner restlessness
industrious	rash
go-ahead	premature
full of initiative	lacking restraint
lively	aimless
engaging	volatile, flighty
spirited	bored

Slow writing

deliberate	slow
thinks before acting	lazy
calm	indecisive
steady	inhibited
prudent	dull
balanced	suspicious

Speed-rating chart

It is possible to time handwriting, although this gives you little information about a person's character. Here is an approximate guide:

slow writing: fewer than 90 letters per minute;
balanced writing: approximately 130 letters per minute;
fast writing: approximately 150 letters per minute;
hyperactive writing: more than 200 letters per minute.

At exams an average senior pupil is expected to write a sentence of ± 18 words, of which ¼ are multi-syllabic, per minute, during a period of at least ½ hour. Girls are quicker than boys.

However, timing is not a method favoured by handwriting analysts, for the reasons given above. They use speed-rating charts to quantify the factors that spur or hamper a writer's progress towards the goal.

A speed-rating chart is printed on p.98. When you analyse a handwriting sample for speed, note each characteristic and allocate it a quickness value and a slowness value on a scale ranging from 0 to 1, in quarterly divisions (this is the scale used in some professional graphology examinations). The quickness value and the slowness value must add up to 1.

For example, when grading degree of connectedness, a sample with no connections at all should be allocated 0 for speed and 1 for slowness; one in which there are connections between the words, as well as the letters, should be allocated 1 for speed and 0 for slowness; and one in which the connections are normal — an average of four letters in a word are connected — should be allocated ½ in each column. Handwriting that falls just above and just below the norm would therefore be allocated ¼ and ¾ in the relevant columns.

When you have finished your allocations, add them up: the total will give you a clear indication as to whether the writer

Speed-Rating Chart

Example

	Slow	*Quick*	
Disconnected letters	$\frac{1}{2}$	$\frac{1}{2}$	Connectedness (4 letters or more)
Connections, angular, arcade, copy-book	$\frac{1}{2}$	$\frac{1}{2}$	Garlands or thready connections
Narrow writing and covering strokes	$\frac{1}{4}$	$\frac{3}{4}$	Broad writing
Pressure heavy, pasty	$\frac{1}{2}$	$\frac{1}{2}$	Pressure light, rhythmic
Regular writing	$\frac{1}{2}$	$\frac{1}{2}$	Irregular writing
'i' dots and 't' bars to left or exact. Breaks in script in order to place them.	$\frac{1}{4}$	$\frac{3}{4}$	'i' dots and 't' bars to right, omitted or connected to further letter
Left margin narrowing or exact	1	0	Left margin widening
Slant: left with leftward tendencies (LT)	$\frac{3}{4}$	$\frac{1}{4}$	Slant: right with rightward tendencies (RT)
Starting strokes and shortened end strokes	$\frac{1}{4}$	$\frac{3}{4}$	No starting strokes and end strokes extended
Writing enriched, precise	$\frac{1}{4}$	$\frac{3}{4}$	Simplicity or neglect
Lines descending	$\frac{1}{4}$	$\frac{3}{4}$	Lines ascending
Strokes wavering, shaky, disintergrating	0	1	Stroke quality firm, with currency
Total	5	7	=12

of your sample is slow, about average, fast or hyperactive. Page 131 gives a blank speed-rating chart for you to copy for repeated use in analyses.

Personal pronoun 'I' (p.p.'I')

The way in which a writer uses 'I' to mean 'me' (that is, 'I' as a personal pronoun as opposed to a capital I as part of another word; graphologists refer to this as p.p.'I') gives the analyst a direct route to the ego. It is unique to the English language. When looking at a handwriting sample, you should consider, for instance: does the p.p.'I' stand upright and on its own, indicating independence, or isolated and slanted to the left, suggesting withdrawal or anxiety?

The answer lies in its relation to the rest of the writing: is it bigger or written with greater pressure? If so, does this indicate self-confidence or do other characteristics in the writing confirm any of its possible stories — an inferiority complex over-compensated; a pretence to create an impression; a mask, indicating an over-sized persona; a defensive/protective zone around an easily injured ego?

Embellishment, and variance with the rest of the writing, show a degree of vanity or presumed self-importance.

A p.p.'I' that fluctuates in size symbolizes the writer's fluctuating self-esteem.

Consider, when interpreting a p.p.'I', the shape of the letter. A distorted p.p.'I' indicates deep-seated inner trouble. Consider the slant of the writing, and the leftward or rightward tendencies (*see* p.58); zonal symbolism (*see* p.56) also obviously applies.

After comparing the p.p.'I's in several samples, the leaders are clearly distinguishable from the subordinates.

Connections

Degree of connectedness

We call writing 'connected' if four or more successive letters in a word are joined, 'disconnected' if fewer than four are joined. High I.V. writing that is well connected indicates logical habits of thinking — one thought develops from another. If the script is wide as well, the writer is entertaining and well adjusted. People with well-developed associative powers combine letters easily; this trait is especially strong

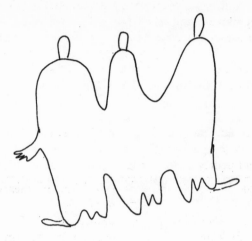

if the 'i' dots are connected. It points to an easy, agile train of thought — a versatile mind, reaching and connecting parts that others do not reach — and superb organizing ability.

Writing that is connected but childish points to lack of originality and restricted ideas.

Extreme connectedness — writing in which words are joined together — can result from a state of continuous over-excitement. This is the writing of a compulsive talker unstoppably boiling over, possibly fending off painful responses or critical appraisal from an unhappily detained listener, who is too polite to interrupt the avalanche.

Large, unrelated gaps at the interconnections of letters in words point to instability and easily provoked irritation. Fragmentation of letters and large, irregular distances between letters in words show up the possibility of disorder in the thinking processes, and problems of adaptation.

Disconnected writing that has been 'welded' by retouching, thus improving readability, may indicate an urge for clarity and an added effort to adapt. However, depending on other signs in the writing, it could indicate a finicky disposition, anxiety, fatigue or stress.

Air lifts

Air lifts, also called air-strokes or air-bridges, are forms of connection that are not really visible, merely indicated. They are, literally, bridges traced in the air by the pen between two letters or two words. For example, a writer might finish a word with an upstroke and barely lift the pen from the paper before beginning the next word with a continuation of that same upstroke.

Air lifts may be perceived as signs of creative imagination, intuition, originality and the ability to take a bird's-eye view. In a disconnected script, if the writer cannot link the letters by an unseen air lift, the train of thought is rather jumpy.

POSITIVE   NEGATIVE

Connected writing

adaptable	lack of independence
logical	dogmatic
able to combine ideas	unoriginal
playful thinking	tending to conform
	subordinate
	one-sided
	narrow-minded
	compulsive

Disconnected writing

ingenious	uncoordinated thinking
quick-witted	illogical
original	unpredictable
intuitive	unable to adapt

Forms of connection

Letters can be joined in four basic ways:

garland: angular:

arcade: thread:

The way in which letters are connected is of great importance for the assessment of character structure. It shows the writer's behaviour in relationships with other people.

GARLAND CONNECTION

In this form of connection, the letters 'm' and 'n' resemble the letter 'u' — they give the impression of having been written upside-down, resembling a cup or bowl. Garland writing flows easily and quickly; garlands originate from supple, gliding movements, which emanate from the suppleness and considerate attitude of the writer. Garlands are directed away from the body, towards others.

Garland writers are natural, open in behaviour and sociable. They dislike conflict and aim for a pleasant atmosphere. They usually know how to strike the right note. They accommodate differences and soon make up with someone after difficulties. They can put themselves in someone else's shoes. Their engaging nature and understanding of others' problems, and their prowess at making contacts, are an ideal basis for a career in the social professions, and also for positions in which arbitration and conciliation are important.

However, it is important not to analyse garland handwriting in too restricted a sense. As always, do not draw conclusions on the basis of one characteristic alone. We analysed the writing of several accountants and, despite the garlands in their writing, found them not all sweetness and light. They exhibited a first-class capacity for penetrating, absorbing and structuring complex data, and reconciling the interests of clients and their bankers.

Garland connections in low I.V. writing signify that the writer is easily influenced; charm may be replaced by weakness.

ARCADE CONNECTIONS

Arcade writing requires more effort than garland writing. Its architectural form makes it slower to execute. Buildings and systems are not constructed overnight. Against the simplicity of garland writing, contrast the affectation of arcade connections: vaulted arches symbolize cover rather than openness, also seclusion and keeping feelings private.

48 Oakleigh Park South
London N20 9JN

Simplified, arcade connection, UZ RT, air lift.

It is difficult to get under the skin of arcade writers. They lack the spontaneity to open up for others and show their real feelings, so they are reserved and do not give anything away. Other people are usually presented with a façade based on pride, intended to impress the outer world. An arcade writer who is power-hungry can produce impressive results.

Arcade writers do not really adapt to others. They are self-absorbed and independent, and they have a strong belief in their own abilities. They are driven by pride to create and achieve, compose and build. Many creative people are arcade writers.

In arcade writers, adaptation is put on — their apparently conformist behaviour is not the real person within. It is sometimes possible to trace a mental resistance to the opinions and influence of others back to a degree of repression in adolescence. A blocking of spontaneity within the family or at school can result in a personality given to conventional politeness: the teenager will listen, but go his or her own way. However, arcades occurring in slow, unstable script with a weak rhythm indicate hypocrisy: politeness become transparent flattery.

Where is the borderline between creative imagination, pretence, hypocrisy and dishonesty? Dr Pulver found arcades prominent in the handwriting of criminals, especially con-men. However, these qualities are difficult to pinpoint in a person's handwriting and facile judgement should be avoided.

Soloist

ANGULAR CONNECTIONS

Angular connections.

Angular writing requires stop and start, abrupt and rigid movements. Precision is needed and this slows the writing movement. The straight, angular lines create a distinct, hard, businesslike impression, indicating effort and energy. Life is not easy, but hard-edged for this writer, who does not shun resistance, but thrives on it, even to the extent of provoking conflict.

Angular writers with good I.V. script are trustworthy; you can rely on their word and build on it. They do not lack self-discipline, are goal-directed and straightforward. Inner tension drives them to develop their abilities. A heavy workload is a challenge to be tackled energetically. Others are stimulated by their pushing power and relentless drive.

Angular writers with low I.V. script find it difficult to adapt. A rigid script indicates lack of compassion, hardness and ruthlessness.

The writer with an angular but regular script is much more stable than the thread writer trying to maintain a precarious balance on the tightrope. However, the latter often scores in creativity and versatility.

THREAD CONNECTIONS

Thread connections.

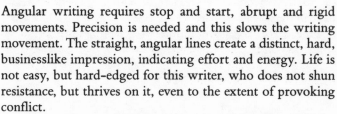

Thready writing looks snake-like; it is quick and sliding. The letters in the middle of words diminish towards the baselines, and often end as a meaningless thread. Form is replaced by movement, energy is preserved, effort is minimized, obstacles are avoided.

Thready writers make social contacts easily. They rarely have head-on clashes with people, rather resorting to evasion, suppleness, diplomacy and cunning. They are often to be found sitting on the fence. Thready writers are born actors suited to many roles. They are chameleons sensitive to the vibrations of their environment, the people around them and circumstances. They are instinctive, good all-rounders, multi-faceted people.

High I.V. writing with thread connections is often found in gifted writers, musicians, actors, diplomats and psychologists.

Thread forms in weak and irregular writing point to spineless and unpredictable behaviour or to lack of personality. If there are also signs of unreliability, the writer may well use natural empathy to mislead.

POSITIVE	NEGATIVE

Garland connections

adaptable, receptive	indecisive
sociable	suggestible
spontaneous	easily distracted
sympathetic	too easy
affable	
relaxed	
confidential	

Arcade connections

closed	reserved
independent	calculating
thinks before acting	artificial
worthy	autocratic
superior, protective	insincere
prudent	haughty

Angular writing

stable	hard
masculine	relentless
resolute	arrogant
disciplined	rigid, not for turning
decisive	unadaptable
straightforward	obstinate
energetic	inconsiderate

Thread writing

with strong pressure	irregular with weak pressure
good all-roundert	lack of personality
talented	spineless
understanding	suggestible
adaptable	unscrupulous
good judge of character	artificial
adroit	two-faced
	keeps sitting on the fence

The stroke

Embellishment and simplicity

The originality the writer shows in forming letters is one of the three factors to consider in establishing the quality — the I.V. level (*see* p.59) — of a handwriting sample. To assess the originality of a writer's letter forms, first consider whether the letters are embellished or simplified. Writing can be embellished by additions to the examples from which you learned to write at school. In simplified writing, inessential parts of letters are omitted.

Embellishment.

Embellishment is an urge to design. In high I.V. writing imagination, receptivity and expressiveness go hand in hand. The script looks enriched by the embellishments, as a result of the writer's sense of beauty.

On the negative side, embellishment can originate from vanity, a tendency to be theatrical or sensational or to exaggerate. When the pressure is also strong, the writer wants to impress. Curls indicate ostentation: appearance is all-important.

Simplifying letters without impairing their legibility shows concise thinking and the ability to separate essentials from side issues.

A few lines to let you know that we be on holiday next week.

We are going to Sicily, to have a

Intelligent and educated people with well-developed reading skills have little difficulty with simplified script because they have more affinity with it, and because they are more familiar with deviations from conventional copybook patterns. Someone who is not used to reading and writing is only used to copybook script and may find it hard to read simplified writing.

Simplification: intelligent, simplified, legible writing. This writing shows analytical skill and intuition, receptivity and critical ability.

This does not mean that people with clear, readable writing are socially superior. The readable but childish writing of an educated person could be a screen. It could signpost lack of independence, clinging to the example of others, or immaturity, regardless of age.

Simplification degenerating into neglect results in throwing out the baby with the bath water. Temporary hurry or impatience can impair legibility in quick, simplified writing. In medium to slow script, simplifications impairing legibility point to inaccuracy and sometimes lack of consideration for others. If you write in a way that others find difficult to read, a certain lack of consideration is implied. It springs from your social tuning and attitude.

POSITIVE	NEGATIVE

Embellished writing

creative	over-estimates side issues
feeling for style and form	artificial
good at portrayal	laborious
descriptive	pretentious
sense of beauty	pompous

Simplified writing

concise thinker	slipshod
good taste	lacks feeling or
perceptive	appreciation for forms
objective	hasty
	impatient

Full or lean letter forms

In full, rich writing, loops, ovals and curves are wide and mainly round forms:

a b g

Writing is lean or meagre if loops and other rounded parts of letters are squashed flat:

a b g

In a script with a good I.V., full writing gives evidence of imagination and the ability to express oneself. In the lower I.V. writing of a less intelligent person, it shows a drift towards fantasizing and exaggeration.

Full writing is associated with warmth of feeling and a sense of humour. Full writers are people who exude an atmosphere of excitement and expectation. They are visual people and retain vivid memories of their visual experiences. Their urge to create goes hand in hand with artistic ability, a talent for design and a sense of style. Their creative intuition is fired by the association of images and ideas.

Advertising agencies and other companies in the creative field need people with what is termed 'psychodynamic tension' — the tension between the conscious and the subconscious mind. This tension comes into play in brainstorming sessions, in which participants bounce ideas off each other, causing vibrations, until, like a flash of

Brainstorming

lightning, parts of the subconscious are discharged into the conscious mind, creating ideas. Full writers are most likely to participate in this, the creative experience.

Lean writing with a high I.V. indicates lucidity and a curious, critical mind. Lean writers like concrete facts and the realistic aspects of everyday life. They apply common sense. Many technicians are lean writers. Lean writers with lower I.V. levels and zonal variations (a small upper zone, for example) may be rather limited in interests and behaviour. If the imagination is underdeveloped, the lean writer's thinking may have become schematic, set in its ways, dry, barren and boring.

POSITIVE   NEGATIVE

Full writing

playful imagination	dreamer
can improvise	fantasist
conceptual imagination	not critical
sensitive	unquestioning
	pretentious
	exaggerated

Lean writing

bright	unimaginative
lucid	one-sided
critical	sober, no sense of humour
modest	dry, dull
penetrating	inhibited
analytic	

Pastose or sharp script

If a fountain pen is gripped near the nib when writing, the flow of ink is reduced slightly, resulting in a sharper, more precise writing than results when the pen is held away from the nib. The more generous ink flow caused by holding the pen higher up on the barrel makes the ink trail spread slightly, so the stroke is less sharp. This less defined writing is termed by graphologists 'pastose' or 'pasty'.

Many painters hold a pen high up, like a brush, so the writing of many artists is pastose. The artistic temperament is, in fact, characteristic of pastose writers: they generally behave in ways that are natural, original and uninhibited. They allow their creativity to surface without too much restraint. The writing of a perceptive person with a penchant for sensual enjoyment — a *bon viveur* — will be pastose.

If the script is deteriorated, having become blotchy and mushy, the writer lacks self-discipline and the power of discernment. Given the sensual susceptibility of the pastose writer, this might indicate a person given to extravagant behaviour, excess or even perverted behaviour.

Such features are especially likely to indicate disaster if there are also indications in the writing of excessive use of alcohol or drugs (*see* p.115, **Warning signs**).

Sharp writing indicates that reason rules over instinct. Writing with the pen held near the nib requires more discipline and pen-control. In a good level I.V. script this corresponds with a critical attitude and evidence of inherent discipline. In a lower I.V. level, the indications are lack of healthy erotic sensitivity and imagination. Thus, sharp writing, sarcasm and caustic wit are closely related.

POSITIVE	NEGATIVE

Pastose writing

original	lack of self-discipline
informal	coarse
loves colour	self-indulgent
healthy eroticism	easily tempted

Sharp script

disciplined	dry
self-assured	cool
determined	sarcastically inclined
critical	judgemental
discerning	lacks healthy eroticism
shrewd	

Addressing the world

The signature

No single area in the field of handwriting has been more abused and vandalized by charlatans and would-be graphologists than the signature. In fact, the conclusions you can draw from a person's signature alone are limited. The signature is not exempt from the cardinal rule of handwriting analysis: that no feature is significant except in relation to others. A great deal is revealed, however, when the signature is compared with the writer's script and its characteristic features.

The signature is a person's public side: a symbolic visiting card, the way he or she wants to appear to the world. It is fascinating to see how people's professional identity or their innermost feelings, are depicted in their signature. For example, a tailor might make an 'X' in his or her signature look like a pair of scissors; an accountant might make certain letters look like figures; musicians might introduce musical symbols. Similarly, a deeply frustrated or over-erotic person might make a capital 'P' look like breasts or a penis.

If the signature is an extension of the script and similar to the rest of the text, the writer is not hiding behind a name plate. He is, in his signature, what he appears to be in his script. This points to an unaffected person, someone who doesn't put on airs.

On the other hand, significant differences between text and signature indicate a discrepancy between form (in the sense of behaviour, appearance and expression) and content, the writer's real nature.

If the signature is larger than the writing, the writer is posing. This can signify a desire to impress or to create a shield against external influences. In fact, such writers are showing off; they may be more modest than they appear.

A signature that is smaller than the writing shows up a writer who may be less modest than otherwise appears — in this case the conclusion is contrary to the obvious. Check for other signs in the writing.

Signature with the movement of a conductor – Sir John Maudwell. This is a professional signature of great individuality, showing directing, supervising, organizing, and planning ability, as well as balance, warmth and vision.

Right: Musical interest.

Far right: Footballer.

The painter Rubens' signature: sensual forms.

Picasso's signatures: simplification, image projection.

Ben Shahn: artist's signature showing graphic quality and beauty.

In handwritten letters the left-right symbolism is expressed in the placing of the signature: generally speaking, the further to the left, the more withdrawn and inhibited the writer; the more to the right, the more outgoing and spontaneous the writer. However, business people often place their signature in line with the left-hand margin, either because they were taught to do so or because it seems a natural position in a typed letter. This example shows how careful you need to be in making interpretations and why it is important not to jump to conclusions based on a single feature. When analysing a handwriting sample for occupational purposes, you should take the candidate's c.v. into consideration.

In a signature, simplicity is an important clue as to character. Attention-seeking and vanity show in superfluous additions or in extra enlargement. If a signature is both oversized and ornate, conceit and mediocrity are blatant or masked in the signer. Modesty will be modest in its movement and its use of space.

It has been the practice for centuries for Englishwomen to drop their maiden name when marrying. Some consider this a loss of identity and even an act of submission. Some women therefore prefer to use Ms instead of Mrs or Miss as an anti-discriminatory measure. Continental married women often sign their own, as well as their husband's name, for example, L. Bal-Baring. This practice sometimes symbolizes a declaration of continued independence: 'I am still myself.'

Embellishment

A wife who writes her husband's name smaller or less clearly than her own is stating that she is her own person and that you must deal with her. She may also not be all that happy with him. The way she expresses his and her name in this connection is telling. It shows her feelings about the marriage. It could also be saying that her personal life is nothing to do with the job.

Women, children and artists frequently write out their Christian name in full; it has a more intimate significance than the surname. It is also the most familiar name. Since early childhood the way it was pronounced, called or thundered identified the speaker, and elicited in the addressed any of a whole gamut of moods, from happiness to anxiety. The artist's signature can also be very personal — an expression of the inner self. However, embellished or extra-large Christian names spell out vanity or a rather innocent mentality, a narcissistic urge to attract attention.

A signature that is wider than the rest of the writing shows the writer's need for space to fulfil an urge for self-expansion. When narrow writing appears only in the signature, the writer reacts in a reserved or inhibited way when under personal attack or when subjected to assessment or even mild criticism. If arcade letter forms appear in a signature with garland connections (*see* p.101), the writer will seem more spontaneous than he really is. In the case of arcade connections with garland letter forms, the writer will be more spontaneous than she appears at first sight.

Business people who sign many cheques, contracts and other documents often deform their signature to render forgery more difficult. In such a case, the body of writing in the text above it must be taken to be predominant in importance.

A full stop after a signature in a sample of good I.V. writing points to prudence. If the writer has been subjected to persecution, as happened, for example, in continental Europe during World War II and in Nazi Germany and the former Communist countries, initial prudence may have solidified into inherent distrust.

Some family members ring the doorbell in their particular way, immediately recognized by the clan; the Masons, members of a well-known secret society, place a dot under their signatures.

If the last stroke of the word goes through the signature, there is dissatisfaction, hostility towards the Self.

No one teaches people to underline their signature.

Individuals who underline are acting from the subconscious — underlining their own rules and the need for power and authority.

If an underlined signature is followed by a full stop, the signer is saying 'That's it!' Add elements like light, increasing or heavy pressure, and embellishment or lack of it, and the signature reveals emotions ranging from vanity and narcissism to decisiveness and unyielding self-defence.

Strokes over the name point to protective feelings for others, but also to caution, concentration and limitation. Horizontal expansion limits vertical expansion.

A signature is a feast for analysis and interpretation, combining, for example, an individual approach, gusto and discipline.

The address

As the title of this section implies, the way a letter is addressed has much in common with the signature, except that legibility is more important. Apply the left-right symbolism of space. Other features may be interpreted as in any sample of handwriting.

Warning signs

Illness, drink or drugs

People suffering from cerebral disorders, such as multiple sclerosis, and spinal disorders, experience disability in varying degrees with the co-ordination of body movements. This causes ataxia — disorderly writing.

Excessive use of drugs or alcohol leads to loss of motor control. Different letters take on the same forms — see 'p' and 'h' and 'l', 'e', 'i'.

Psychotics and schizophrenics may share certain symptoms with alcoholics and drug addicts, perhaps caused by their treatment. The analyst should tactfully enquire, in case of doubt, about legitimate use of drugs — along with questions about eyesight and use of spectacles, for example.

In this section of the book we deal with the manifestations in handwriting of drink and drug abuse, and the illnesses described above. Indications of physical illness also show in handwriting, but these medical aspects of graphology are beyond the scope of this book, and are best left to the researchers and practitioners in that field.

GENERAL POINTS

Look out for granulated, coarse, rope-like strokes, irregular pressure, signs of weak sense of self (a small or distorted p.p.'I') and increasingly immature writing (regression to school writing).

The effect of drink and drugs on people at work is of direct concern to employers and colleagues. The writing movement originates from the brain; alcohol works in stages, first apparently stimulating, but soon sapping, like a creeping paralysis, the strength and the condition of the individual.

Some drugs and sustained alcohol misuse cause instant highs and long-term after-effects. Handwriting — that permanent distillation of a great many body movements — cannot fail to register the deterioration of concentration, cohesion and control. Alcohol is still the most widespread source of problems at work.

Stages of intoxication and the consequences on the ink trail

Early stage	Consequences in the script
Mood change: merry, more jovial, spontaneous, fewer inhibitions.	Script increases in size and width; more curls, swings, jutting strokes, and other embellishments.
Increased feeling of self-esteem may lead to overestimation of self, the inflated ego syndrome.	Larger capitals, more embellishment. Proportions of size strongly changeable. Direction of the down-strokes becomes irregular.

Advanced stage

Early symptoms reinforced. Co-ordination of movements disturbed. Swaying walk. Arm movements become unsure, missing aim occasionally.

Increased lack of rhythm and regularity. Wavering lines. Ataxic and broken strokes. Lack of motor control causes increased jutting strokes and darting out of the pen.

Speech difficulties cause lack of clarity and comprehensibility. Faculty of thought suffers interference. Ability to concentrate becomes unstable. Strong disturbance of equilibrium.

Decreasing legibility. Some letters become look-alikes ('h' may become 'p' or 'n'. for example). Parts of letters, whole letters, and words are added or missing. Crossing out, transposing letters in a word, slips of the pen all increase, leading to illegibility. Lines falling, sometimes steeply, reflecting disturbance of equilibrium.

Dishonesty

Employers obviously want to know about *risk* factors in connection with prospective employees. Indicators in handwriting for dishonesty are shown below. To misinterpret signs of dishonesty in a candidate's handwriting would be such a terrible injustice, however, that you must take the greatest possible care in your analysis. You may have to defend your opinion at an industrial tribunal or in court. Always bear these points in mind:

- Some of the following trends can be observed at times in almost any handwriting. Only if at least four or five indications reappear frequently in the same script should you contemplate a conclusion of possible dishonesty, of risk.
- Slow writing is an essential ingredient in justifying a negative conclusion. If the writing is lively and spontaneous, the likelihood of dishonesty is diminished dramatically. Consider this: what is bribery in one country or context is commission in another. Morals differ.

Saudek, Pulver and several other experts[1] pinpoint the following indications for unreliability and related defects:

1. Slow writing.
2. Artificial, stylized or characterless 'copybook' script.
3. Unnecessary retouches which do not improve legibility.
4. Letters looking like other letters (an 'a' and an 'o' might look like the same letter, for example, so might an 'r' and a 'v').

'a' and 'o'   *'r' and 'v'*

5. Initial emphasis, frequent interruptions and many letters inserted in the place of other letters.
6. Ovals or circles in the letters 'a', 'b', 'd', 'g', 'o', 'q' open at the base (thus written in two strokes with a left-turning movement).

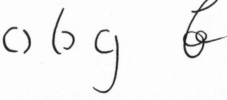

7. Capital letters disproportionate in size – that is, in relation to the middle zone letters.
8. Excessive dotting and punctuation. Resting point dots.
9. Fragmented letters with parts missing, in combination with slowness in a developed script.
10. Wavy, erratic base lines, 'spineless' instability of the script and thread forms.
11. Strong leftward tendencies.
12. Strokes that are slack and muddy.
13. Displaced pressure. Normal pressure is downward; pressure is displaced if it is where you do not expect to find it – on the right-hand side of a long 't' bar, for example.
14. Malformed or small personal pronoun 'I' (p.p.'I').

Spineless character.

[1]Nos. 1–10 Saudek/Pulver; 6 and 12 Crepieux-Jamin; 11 and 12 Teillard-Mendelssohn; 12 Prof. Pophal; 13 and 14 Link.

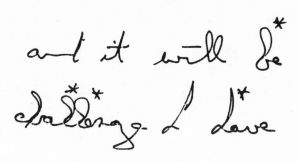

'Spineless' letters.

Deliberate concealment

While the graphologist deals with character, the handwriting expert working in a legal context has to appear in court or at an industrial tribunal as an expert witness to defend an opinion on questions such as who wrote a certain contested signature, whether two signatures were written by the same person or whether additions to, say, a petty cash voucher are forged. To become a contested document expert requires years of study and much experience. Falsified expense accounts, altered agreements, anonymous and poison pen letters, forged signatures on cheques and other documents, are, therefore, a separate area of expertise. It is one that is particularly fascinating. Specialist experts may report on fingerprinting or chemical detection work, but these aspects of technical analysis are beyond the scope of this book.

There are, however, recognizable faultline factors that may be detected in a questioned document, and these are set out below. If you have reason to suspect anyone of deliberate concealment and you detect several of these signs in his or her handwriting, it is essential that the handwriting be independently examined by an expert analyst.

A high I.V. writing can never be produced by a lower I.V. level writer, but low I.V. writing can sometimes be reproduced by a high I.V. writer. However, with increasing text or increasing speed, a relapse into familiar style is almost unavoidable, so the culprit can be detected by the characteristic features of his or her script. Signs of the forger's script or slow writing — a necessary feature when copying — plus combinations of the 12 points listed above, play an important part in the detection of an individual engaged in these activities.

People often think that changing a script is fairly simple. In fact, identification does not present great difficulties in the majority of cases if there is enough comparative material.

Most anonymous letter-writers show little imagination in masking their identity. They change the slant of the letters and the size or shape of capital letters or they write in capitals. Many characteristic features of their own script remain unchanged, because they are not aware of them. The way the 't's are crossed or the 'i's dotted, the pressure, the distance between words or letters, the balance of the small letters in relation to the upper and lower loops — all these are giveaways.

The expert knows what it is easiest to change or imitate, where the initial hard work can be expected, and where difficulties may arise and lapses of concentration are most likely to occur.

The experts at Graph-O-Logica who deal with forgeries, such as unauthorized alterations to contracts, forged cheques and other legal work, have noticed since the early 1980s a steady increase in requests for help with tracing the writers of poison pen letters around Christmas. With the seasonal greetings goes an increase in nastiness, apparently. They have also noticed an increased wave of work involving tracking down people who have ordered a stream of goods in someone else's name.

Recently a company was plagued by the addition of obscene messages to women customers, written in capitals. Fortunately, it was company policy to ask every employee to fill in a detailed card annually. This enabled comparison of 150 handwriting samples to be made by an expert, so that the person responsible was flushed out.

Poison pen.

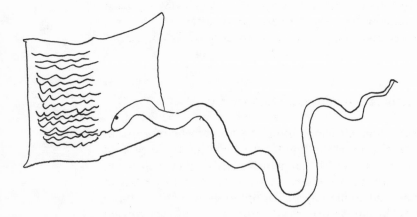

4 Analysis and Report

The work you have done so far may be regarded as the preliminary sketch from which the portrait of a writer is built up. The next stage involves applying the colour. However, you must always remember that a square of colour takes on different tones and shades when it is put next to other colours. A single note becomes music only in association with other notes. In handwriting analysis, as in music or painting, only the whole — the sum total of the parts — conveys meaning. None of the handwriting characteristics you have noted can have any significance unless it is considered in association with others.

What you have assembled so far is a number of measurements and observations recorded on your Check List. How do these basic elements fit together to make a portrait of a person?

Determining the I.V. level (*see* p.59) has provided you with a key, but this key only unlocks the door to the personality by giving you a clue as to whether a feature indicated in a person's handwriting should be given a positive or a negative interpretation. The next stage is to pinpoint the most important of the many different features and their associated interpretations that you have noted on your Check List.

Prominent features: Dominants

In every person's handwriting there are certain prominent features that recur throughout the script, like the key, beat and tempo in music. In handwriting analysis, these recurring features are called *dominants*. A particular slant (*see* p.89) is an obvious and commonly occurring dominant.

How do you discover the dominants in your handwriting sample? Search through it for the following features:

slant
absolute size of the script
zonal size distribution (the order of domination of each of the
    three zones, in terms of size)
layout (margins, etc)
rhythm
pressure
form(s) of connection
degree of connectedness
degree of simplification or embellishment
broadness and/or narrowness
horizontal tension
rightward and/or leftward tendencies
fullness and/or leanness.

You should find between four and six dominants in your
handwriting sample. Note them on your Check List, in order
of prominence. Their relative importance will guide you
when you write your report.

Contrasting features

Because human personality is full of contrasts, it follows that
interpreting these dominant features cannot be as simple as
looking up possible interpretations and noting those that
seem most appropriate. Like the human character, handwriting is full of contradictions. If you study your
handwriting sample again, you should notice contrasting
elements, called *counter-dominants*, that go against the grain,
contradicting the dominants.

For example a rightward slant, indicating a desire for
interaction, may be a dominant feature, while at the same
time, if the word-spacing is wide, a desire to stay aloof is also
indicated — a counter-dominant.

'A dominating contradiction [is] the real source of
personality,' wrote Robert Saudek in *The Psychology of
Handwriting*. If you find the idea of counter-dominants hard
to understand, think of the contradictions that co-exist in
your personality. You can love *and* hate, depending on the
circumstances. You can laugh *and* weep.

In a handwriting sample, the dominants are the important —
the telling — features; the counter-dominants carry less
weight. Indeed, a handwriting sample will not necessarily
reveal a counter-dominant for every dominant feature.

Nevertheless, in that the counter-dominants counteract the dominant personality features, they are significant.

Like the hues and their complementary colours in a painting, the tension and counter-balance of dominant and counter-dominant traits creates uniqueness and interest in a personality.

Look for contradictory aspects of personality in the script you are analysing. To do this, look through your Check List for features that contradict the dominant character traits you have listed. For example, if you have 'large overall size' as a dominant feature of your sample, you may have noted under 'pressure' on your Check List that the writing pressure is light (see p.88): you have found a counter-dominant.

As you become experienced at analysing handwriting, pinpointing the dominants and counter-dominants in a sample becomes a faster process. Meanwhile, you can refer to the list of commonly occurring dominants and counter-dominants below. You will come across many more in the course of time. Keep a note of them and see how other indicators bring about subtle variations in the wording of your interpretations.

Note the interpretations of the counter-dominants on your Check List beneath those of the dominants.

Dominants and counter-dominants

Dominant/ Counter-dominant	Interpretation
dominant middle zone/ left slant	wants to interact well, but is holding off, deterring such needs in practice
large capitals/ small middle zone	brisk manner, ambitious attitude and apparent need for success, yet has little ambition
large overall size/ small middle zone	wishes to be a major figure, yet has little need to be involved with others outside the business sphere
large overall size/ clear left slant	needs to be the centre of attention, yet wants privacy

Dominant/ Counter-dominant	Interpretation
large overall size/ light pressure	high-profile behaviour and ambition, but lacks the dynamism to arrive
right slant/ narrowness between downstrokes	extravert behaviour, but selective about involvement with others
right slant/ wide spacing between lines and words	the desire for interaction struggles with the urge to remain dissociated
right slant/ leftward tendencies in the three zones	appears to be a team player, yet self-concerned or selfish
rightward tendencies/ wide right margin	desire for progress, but held back by inner restraints
right slant/ avoidance of right margin	fear of the future, yet readily seeks a challenge
narrow right margin/ narrowing left margin	a basically active and extravert person becoming increasingly cautious over time
right slant/ rightward tendencies with arcade connections	basic ease and ability to relate to others, but needs personal privacy
vertical slant/ rightward tendency	a highly active person barely kept in check by reticence
left slant/ narrow spacing between words	a lone worker at heart, who appears at ease with others

Dominant/ Counter-dominant	Interpretation
large word spacing/ garlands	warm inner glow, receptive, frustrated; caution inhibits outgoing impulse, like mutually repellent magnetic poles
equal speed rating, 6 quick/6 slow	desire to succeed in the fast lane, yet with the brakes on
heavy pressure/ dominant middle zone	hard-headed on the outside, but warmer and softer inside
heavy pressure/ garland connections	firm and aggressive in style, but does not relish a fight
garland connections/ left slant or leftward tendencies	warm and outgoing at heart, but also reserved
light pressure/ angle connections	aggressive thinking, but lacks the guts to be confrontational
angular middle zone/ rounded capitals	iron fist in a velvet glove
small writing/ large signature	usually modest, but not shy of putting on a show
contrasting differences between text and signature	contrast between public and private persona, real self and image, or projected image

Painting a portrait in writing

Allocating the correct interpretation to the dominant and counter-dominant features in your sample is a crucial part of the analysis, since these features are the key to the personality. This, then, is the most taxing part of any analysis, since, as you have already seen, each writing characteristic has many possible meanings, depending on the I.V. The I.V., the dominants and the speed-rating chart are the foundation stones of your analysis. Taking these as your starting point, you can proceed to build on them.

Filling in the details

From your handwriting sample you have selected at most five or six dominants, together with any counter-dominants. Yet your sample is composed of a vast number of features. Those you recorded on your Check List provide the details you use to colour in the sketch of the writer of your sample.

Think of your selected dominants and counter-dominants as the main arguments in a thesis you are writing on the subject of your sample. How can you support these arguments? In your Check List you have noted some features that support the traits indicated in your list of dominants and others that support those in your list of counter-dominants. List them in your notebook, together with their interpretations.

In considering the interpretations of these features, you should begin to glimpse the personality behind the handwriting. This is the key to your analysis.

Compiling clusters

This is the point at which handwriting analysis becomes fascinating. An experienced graphologist will set out from here to reach the core of the personality — a long and difficult process. The graphologist will ponder all the clues in the sample and draw a series of conclusions that will penetrate the deepest recesses of the subject's personality. A full character analysis could be as long as a novel.

It takes years to reach this degree of expertise. You need to speed up and simplify the process, condensing your findings to the essential. Luckily, your task is to consider personality from a specific angle and this makes the job easier. Your context is straightforward: job selection. When progressing to the point where you begin to write your report, always ask yourself: is the person whose handwriting sample you are analysing suitable for a specific job? Then stick to your objective: to draw up an occupational portrait in writing.

This is where a good job description (*see* p.48) becomes a beacon; and why it is important to refer to the candidate's c.v. when making an analysis. You can then compare the characteristics in the handwriting sample with the requirements of the position to be filled.

When doing this, you must still bear in mind that spotting one characteristic and supporting it with another does not mean that you have the key to the writer's character. Personality has a multiplicity of facets and you need a cluster of as many as three to six signs, all pointing in the same direction, before you can be confident that you are being led towards one personality feature. Handwriting analysis is like detective work — there is a mass of seemingly disconnected facts. You have to decide which are important and which are not.

In summary, having listed the dominants and counter-dominants and grouped around them features in your handwriting sample that appear to reinforce the character trait to which they point, you must now evaluate how pronounced these traits might be. That will depend on the evidence you have assembled to support your argument — the strengths or weaknesses of the various characteristics you have clustered around your dominant features. By putting several clusters together, you form patterns from which you gradually construct a picture of the personality, your end result.

Experienced handwriting analysts can spot these clusters of characteristics very quickly and from them form an instant picture of the writer's personality in their mind. In common with all diagnostic sciences, the degree of validity of graphological conclusions depends on the expertise of the analyst's observational skills. Ability and aptitude are important, but above all comes the co-ordinating capacity to synthesize visible signs, like slant, with less obvious and immaterial concepts, like speed.

You, the beginner, have first to evaluate each sign, then studiously piece together the clusters. Learning to do this takes time, and you must treat the learning process with respect. The character traits that handwriting features symbolize are the essence of the personality. To misinterpret them is to misunderstand the person whose handwriting you are analysing, and that may be damaging to him or her.

We have tentatively simplified this process for you by compiling a keyword list of characteristics required for various jobs (based on the **Career pointers** *see* Appendix 5, and clustering beneath them combinations of handwriting characteristics that together point to the given personality trait.

Our keyword list is by no means an exhaustive index of possible clusters: we have selected commonly occurring groups of handwriting characteristics with interpretations likely to be appropriate in candidate selection and other situations relevant to the readers of this book. The clusters are not prescriptions or recipes for an instant interpretation of characteristics. When you come to apply them to handwriting samples, you will find the characteristics in the writing do not fit the clusters in every detail. In such cases you will need to consider your observations very carefully, and produce your own clusters.

The role of perception

It should become clear at this key stage that the process of handwriting analysis is not a simple matter of two plus two equals four. You are not dealing with standard, static entities. Nobody is an island or reacting to an unchanging environment. Intuition, creative thinking and, above all, perception, play a crucial role at this stage. Some tiny sign, conscientiously noted at an early stage, may suddenly take on great significance as a result of the kind of mental leap that led Einstein to deduce that $E = mc^2$.

These dogged steps we have outlined in this chapter can be likened to the first strokes you made with a pencil between ruled lines in a copybook when you first learned to write as a child. The difference between those and the speedy scribblings with which you filled in your Check List are equal to the chasm of time and experience that yawns between your first steps at analysis and the fast observations and deduction of an experienced graphologist. Never forget that you are not yet a handwriting expert. Only with true understanding will you be able to produce an accurate, in-depth portrait of a personality. Achieving that understanding takes time. Graphologists say that after analysing 1,000 letters under supervision, the serious student should show a marked improvement in the speed of analysis without impairing accuracy. Real expertise comes only after the student has analysed several letters a week for three years, while making an intensive study of psychology.

Writing the report

You now have all the information you need to write a report. It is advisable to break up your analysis under a number of headings to avoid repetition. Ours are written under the headings 'Intelligence and personality'; 'Attitude towards work'; and 'Attitude towards others'. You can read our reports with examples in Appendix 5.

It might be useful to bear these suggestions in mind when writing a report:

- Make it easy to read — write it in simple language.
- The opening statement colours the reader's view of the rest. Leave your general summary to the end.
- Stick to what is important to the business. Remember to include a paragraph on any special requirements of the company ('candidate must be adaptable to change as the company is breaking into new markets overseas').
- Avoid intrusion into the candidate's private life, other than those aspects that are relevant to the business.

And one further point to consider: writing the report is the final stage in analysing handwriting, a two-part process. The analysis, the first part, requires observation, memory skills and logic. The second part — the report — involves drawing up a holistic portrait of the writer, and this requires perception and flexible, lateral thinking processes — the making of mental leaps — as was explained in the Introduction.

To return to reality, it is inevitable that not everyone can or would want to become equally good at fathoming out how people tick, and getting to the bottom of the diverse motivations of human behaviour. Not everyone who studies handwriting analysis will want to become a graphologist. But studying the subject will undoubtedly enrich your own personality.

Appendix 1

Check list

Name: LH/RH   Date:
                                                           Date of
                                                           sample:
Company name:

        address: phone:
                                                   fax:

Age: M/F   Our ref: Your ref:

Country where writer learned to write: Any handicap:

Function/Job description/Advert/Training/c.v.:

I.V. Chart
(see pp. 59–62)
A: General layout: Use of space, proportions, balance, harmony.

B: Natural or artificial writing? Form, style, designed, ornate.

C: Originality of letterforms: Mature, simplified, legible, copybook.

Indicate level for A, B, and C in the appropriate place, in one of the squares.

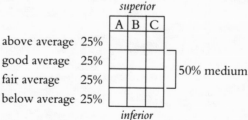

superior

		A	B	C	
above average	25%				
good average	25%				50% medium
fair average	25%				
below average	25%				

inferior

Notes and first impressions on I.V.:

Margins:
(see pp. 65–7)

	wide	*narrow*		*wide*	*narrow*
left upper	☐	☐	right upper	☐	☐
left lower	☐	☐	right lower	☐	☐

left margin:
widening	☐
straight	☐
narrowing	☐
irregular	☐

right margin:
widening	☐
straight	☐
narrowing	☐
irregular	☐

margins and use of space
(for your sketch):

No margins: left ☐   right ☐

Margins like a frame around the text?   yes ☐   no ☐

Notes:

Speed-Rating Chart

	Slow	Quick	
Disconnected letters			Connectedness (4 letters or more)
Connections, angular, arcade, copy-book			Garlands or thready connections
Narrow writing and covering strokes			Broad writing
Pressure heavy, pasty			Pressure light, rhythmic
Regular writing			Irregular writing
'i' dots and 't' bars to left or exact. Breaks in script in order to place them.			'i' dots and 't' bars to right, omitted or connected to further letter
Left margin narrowing or exact			Left margin widening
Slant: left with leftward tendencies (LT)			Slant: right with rightward tendencies (RT)
Starting strokes and shortened end strokes			No starting strokes and end strokes extended
Writing enriched, precise			Simplicity or neglect
Lines descending			Lines ascending
Strokes wavering, shaky, disintergrating			Stroke quality firm, with currency
Total			=12

Grapho-speed:

very slow ☐   slow ☐   quick ☐   very quick ☐

Spacing:
(see pp. 67–71)

Spacing between letters: wide □   medium □   narrow □
                             irregular □   rigid □

Spacing between words: wide □   narrow □
                            balanced □   irregular □

Spacing between lines: wide □   small □   mingling □
                            irregular □   rivers □   *aerated □

(* *balanced distribution between lines and words of black and white*)

Notes:

Line direction: rising □   falling □   straight □   wavy □
(see pp. 71–4)   concave □   convex □   tiled up □   tiled down □

Notes:

Horizontal tension: baseline: taut □   slack □
(see pp. 74–5)

Notes:

Rhythm: good □ harmonious □ fair □ controlled □ irregular □ rigid □
(see pp. 75–7)

Notes:

Zones and zonal dominance:
(see pp. 78–80)

*UK copybook:	UZ	3mm	MZ	3mm	LZ	3mm
sample:	UZ	mm	MZ	mm	LZ	mm

UZ and LZ dominant:		mm	balanced harmony	mm
	erratic	mm	absolute size small 'f'	mm

*In many countries copybook UZ and LZ are extended. What is important is a harmonious balance.

Notes:

Leftward and rightward tendencies in the three zones:
(see pp. 80–1)

LT: ☐ UZ   ☐ MZ   ☐ LZ
RT: ☐ UZ   ☐ MZ   ☐ LZ

Notes:

Initial strokes and letters:
(see pp. 82–4)

Final strokes and letters:
(see pp. 82–4)

Notes:

Pressure:
Examine the script and the back of the page, noting the indent the writer makes on the paper with the pen. (see pp. 88–9)

light	☐	medium	☐	strong	☐
side pressure	☐	pressure/release pattern	☐	spineless	☐
fluctuations	☐	stem: stable	☐	mobile	☐

Notes:

Slant: rightward ☐   leftward ☐   vertical ☐
(see pp. 89–91)   extreme RS/LS ☐   mixed/wavering ☐

Notes: (note the degree of slant)

'i' dots: high ☐   low ☐   leftward ☐   rightward ☐   exact ☐
(see p. 92)   omitted ☐   neglected ☐   connected ☐

Notes:

't' bars: high ☐   low ☐   leftward ☐   rightward ☐   exact ☐   connected ☐
(see p. 92)

Notes:

Personal pronoun 'I' : large ☐   balanced ☐   small ☐   distorted ☐
(see p. 97)   consistent size ☐   slant ☐   pressure ☐   form ☐

Notes:

Degree of connectedness:
(see pp. 97–8)
☐ very connected (more than four letters)
☐ partially connected (varying and three to four letters)
☐ disconnected (mainly fewer than three letters)
☐ air lifts

Notes:

Forms of connection: garlands ☐   arcades ☐   angular ☐   threads ☐
(see pp. 101–6)

Notes:

Embellishment and simplicity: embellished ☐   simplified ☐   neglected ☐   original ☐
(see pp. 106–8)

Notes:

Letter forms: full ☐   lean ☐
(see pp. 108–10)   ovals: open ☐   closed ☐   knotted ☐

Notes:

Stroke quality: pastose ☐   sharp ☐
(see pp. 110–11)

Notes:

Signature:	large ☐	balanced ☐	small ☐	as text ☐
(see pp. 111–15)	ornate ☐	simplified ☐	legible ☐	illegible ☐
	wide ☐	narrow ☐	underlined ☐	full stop ☐

stroke through signature ☐   capitals:
number of disconnections ☐   deviations from text ☐   fluctuations ☐

Notes:

Dominants	*Counter-dominants*
(see pp. 122–5)	
4–6 maximum	
in order of prominence	if any
1.	1.
2.	2.
3.	3.
4.	4.
(5.)	(5.)
(6.)	(6.)

Other observations:

Overall look: round ☐   angular ☐   threaded ☐   mixed ☐

Capital letters: large ☐   balanced ☐   small   ☐

Special letter formations:

Special connections:

Legibility: good   ☐   medium   ☐   low   ☐

Signs of stress: instability ☐   dishonesty ☐   drugs ☐   alcoholism ☐

Notes:

Consider further:

Honesty/risk chart (see pp. 177–8)

Compatibility (where relevant) (see pp. 164–6)

Notes:

Psychological clusters

Traits, characteristics, qualities, positive and negative. An aid to the definition of job requirements, descriptions and multiple-sign analysis.

Many of the character features listed in this appendix are also listed in the Compatibility Chart on page 168.

Accuracy

small middle zone legible well-placed diacritics regular, rhythmic (but either of these features present in excess indicates a tendency toward rigidity or compulsion)	Meticulous attention to detail. A careful and diligent worker.

Adaptability

See also Compatibility Chart, No.9.

fast rhythmic co-ordinated movement balanced fairly regular clever letter combinations well-connected writing, but not over-connected	Adjusts easily to environment and to social situations.

Aggressiveness

angles
left margin wide or widening
word-endings with downward
   tendency
narrow word-spacing
pointed pressure
ascending base lines

Tackles business and private problems
energetically and forcefully, even
abrasively. Argues and acts with
ferocity and drive. Treats business
campaigns as a military assault.
Is the first to attack without
provocation.

Aloofness (Also *Meanness*)

See also Compatibility Chart, No.6.

arcades
vertical or left slant
narrow word-spacing
no end strokes

An aloof personality may show signs
of harshness or meanness or both.
These features are characteristic of
predominantly harsh personality traits.

Altruism

See also Compatibility Chart, No.7.

round, right-slanting, broad writing
garland connections
extended end strokes
absence of rigidity (fluid script;
   variations in downstroke; baseline
   not too taut)

Unselfish attitude and behaviour.

Analytical intelligence

small
regular
angular
simplified
balanced zones, well detailed

The ability to break down complex phenomena into their component parts.

Approachability

rightward tendencies
garlands
moderate middle zone
aerated

Willing to hear the views of others; opens the way to interrelating and exchanging ideas.

Aspiring

dominant-sized upper zone
elaboration in upper zone
ascending or convex base lines
ascending 't' bars

The desire to reach a goal is not necessarily matched by personal abilities or the reality of a situation.

Assertiveness

angles
middle zone dominance
emphasis on capitals/first letters
decisive word finals
and signature

Polite but firm insistence upon recognition of one's claims, declarations and opinions.

Authority

strong pressure
end pressure
large writing
right slant

Based on entrusted power or the need to exercise power. If the writing shows signs of rigidity (e.g., no variation in downstrokes; horizontal tension too taut), the writer is excessively authoritarian.

Boredom, dullness, monotony

See also Compatibility Chart, No.18.

copybook writing, slow
reproduction calligraphic writing
unoriginal
weak
regular

Business acumen (Also *Commercial intuition*)

threads
'i' dots and 't' bars through–connected
   (joined to the following letter)
lower zone emphasis

Caring (Also *Concern for others, Responsibility*)

See also Compatibility Chart, No.18.

garlands
rightward tendencies
middle zone small to moderate
tapering word size
narrow word-spacing

Cleverness

garland roundness
individual forms, such as lassos
undulating base lines
thready connections and word-endings
fluency

Opportunistic use of available means,
circumstances and ideas
(not necessarily one's own). Quick to
perceive ways out, to circumvent
situations and to devise unorthodox
solutions.

Commercial intelligence

strong pressure
angles
rightward tendencies

The ability to recognize and enhance
commercial opportunities and turn
them to profit; to make value
judgements where financial criteria are
a major factor.

Commercial intuition

See Business acumen.

Commitment to duty

modest p.p.'I'
strong 't' bars (will-power)
steady base lines
well-placed 'i' dots and 't' bars
legible signature
regularity

The sense of giving oneself to a task or duties, and the degree of attention paid to them consistently over a period of time.

Communication skills

angularity
right slant
rightward tendencies
rising base lines
varying pressure
narrow letter-spacing

The ability to convey ideas, concepts, orders, instructions, teachings, concisely and lucidly to a variety of people.

Competitiveness

angularity
pressure
vertical or rightward tendencies
exceptional p.p.'I'
strong signature

Striving for supremacy in rivalry against others.

Concentration

See Distraction.

Concern for others

See Caring; Responsibility. *See also* Compatibility Chart, No.13.

Confident self-presentation

reasonably well-formed personal pronoun 'I'
emphasis on first letter
strong 't' bars
strong signature

Independence.
Self-assurance, stemming from self-reliance.

Courtesy

arches, garlands
good layout, well-balanced margins
legibility
regularity

Consideration, graciousness, good manners, ceremoniousness.

Creative intelligence

See also Imagination.

high I.V. with irregularity
simplification, upper zone elaboration
clever individual connections and forms
original inter-zonal fluency
spatially well balanced

Originality, perception and the ability to combine imagination and analytical aptitude or skill to produce useful ideas.

Decisiveness

speed
resolute word finals
angularity
firm pressure
no starting strokes
hooks
stable, uninhibited

The ability to be determined and conclusive, enabling immediate action to be carried out.

Dependability

See Honesty. *See also* Compatibility Chart, No.1.

Depression

descending base lines
variable letter slant
drooping word endings
inconsistency
inharmonious movements

Decrease in activity or reactivity
manifested by lack of purpose, lack of
interest in the pleasures of life,
feelings of inadequacy, despondency,
sadness, pessimism, anxiety.

Dictatorial

angles
downward tendency on last letters
heavy pressure
high 't' bars
tall capitals
narrow word-spacing

A tendency to dominate. An inclination
to command, control and rule over
people and their thinking.

Dishonesty

See Honesty/risk chart, pp.177—8. *See also* Compatibility Chart, No.2.

slow writing
artificial, stylized or characterless
 copybook script
unnecessary retouches, not improving
 legibility
letters looking like other letters
initial emphasis, frequent
 interruptions, and many letters
 inserted in the place of other letters
the ovals in the letters
 'a', 'b', 'd', 'g', 'o', 'q', open at the
 bottom, thus written in two
 strokes, with left-turning
 movement; looped, knotted ovals
 or circles
capital letters disproportionate in size
 with the rest of the writing; uneven
 MZ letters, jutting out
excessive dotting and punctuation
resting point dots
leaving out parts of letters, in
 combination with slowness in a
 developed script
wavy erratic base lines, slack,
 'spineless' script, and thread forms
strong leftward tendencies
slack, muddy strokes
displaced pressure
malformed or small p.p.'I'

Unreliability and related defects.

Caution!
Only if at least four or five
indications reappear in the same
script should you risk contemplating
a conclusion of possible dishonesty.
In such a case it would be necessary
to seek confirmation from an
experienced, qualified graphologist.

Distraction

lack of harmony
height and pressure differences
irregular letter formations
breaks and stops in letters
variances in use of space and slant
downward directional tendencies
sinuous base lines
irregular use of diacritics

Inability to concentrate.

Dogmatism (Also *Inflexibility*)

See also Compatibility Chart, No.10.

angles
heavy downstrokes
decisive word-endings
rigidity

Domineering

See Dictatorial.

Drive

See Power, need for.

Dynamism

fast writing
no starting strokes
rightward tendencies
large writing
rising baseline

Empathy

See also Compatibility Chart, No.5.

garlands
rightward tendencies
flexible or thready finals
medium or small middle zone

The ability to stand in someone else's shoes and see things from their point of view, without necessarily agreeing.

Energy, vitality

mild to firm pressure
rightward tendencies
widening left margin
fast writing
supple base line

Enthusiasm

rightward tendencies
ascending base lines
diverse, expressive freedom
pressure
strong ascending 't' bars

Contagious excitement for a project, subject or cause. (Note that 'expressive freedom' means that the writer diverts from copybook script in a variety of ways and forms.)

Extraversion

speed
no starting strokes
rightward tendencies
simplification
significant middle zone

Outward-directedness towards people, goals, objects, ideas, situations.

Flexibility

garlands, some angularity
speed
varied degrees of connectedness and
    unconnectedness
clever combinations
fluency
threading

The ability to adjust, to cope with change, with having one's proposals modified and adapted by others, including producing — and working with — compromise.

Fluency

speed
simplification
interzonal balance
legibility
fluency
individual forms

Ease and lucidity in communicating, both in writing and verbally.

Friendliness (Also *Generosity, Humour, sense of*)

garland connections
round writing
full, broad writing with rightward
   tendencies
extended open curved end strokes
good spacing and margins
quick, lively
conventional types: with arcades

Generosity

See Friendliness. *See also* Compatibility Chart, No.1 and Honesty/risk chart, pp. 177–8.

Harshness

See Aloofness; Meanness. *See also* Compatibility Chart, No.6.

Honesty (Also *Dependability, Reliability and related characteristics*)

See also Compatibility Chart, No.1 and Honesty/risk chart, pp. 177–8.

quick, spontaneous, regular and
   rhythmic writing
constant pressure
firm and lively strokes
legible, well-detailed forms, with
   diacritics
healthy tension, good balance and
   proportions throughout script
signature and script related

Caution!
Honesty is a value concept, subject to
cultural and circumstantial
variations

Humour, sense of

See Friendliness; Imagination.

Imagination (Also *Humour, sense of*)

See also Creative intelligence; Compatibility Chart No.17.

---

upper zone elaboration
playful vertical or horizontal strokes
curvy, round, wavy forms
creative, original and full forms
loops and ovals well shaped

Immaturity (Also *Indecision*)

See also Compatibility Chart No.12.

---

increasing word size
varying letter slant
awkward connections and
    co-ordination
preponderance of strokes over letters

The script gives an overall impression
of lots of lines.

Indecision (Also *Immaturity*)

See also Compatibility Chart, No.12.

---

hesitant, unstable, weak writing

Independence

See also Confident self-presentation.

---

upright slant
good-sized p.p.'I'
movement contrary to copybook
emphasis on first letters
strong 't' bars
strong signature

Inflexibility (Also *Dogmatism*)

See also Compatibility Chart, No.10.

consistent slant, size, spacing
angles, heavy downstrokes
decisive terminals
rigidity, tautness

Ingenuity (Also *Resourcefulness*)

high I.V. with irregularity
upper zone elaboration
relatively large upper zone
some angularity
creative, original forms
simplified, spatially well balanced script

Creative use of connections,
personnel and materials. Ability to
cope imaginatively during
emergencies.

Initiative

speed
simplification
rightward tendencies
no or short starting strokes
original forms

Taking the first step; taking the lead
without prompting; setting a process
into motion; proceeding with purpose.

Insensitivity (to social environment) (Also *Irresponsibility*)

See also Compatibility Chart, No.14.

left slant
flat, low garlands, but without
    garland finals

Insincerity

See also Compatibility Chart, No.2.

covering strokes
marked differences between text and
    signature
letters written in an odd direction

Integrity

See also Compatibility Chart, No.7.

regularity	Incorruptibility, commitment to fair play, truth and professional ethics.
simplification	
legibility	
dominant upper zone	
no excesses	

Intelligence

See also Analytical intelligence; Commercial intelligence; Creative intelligence; Productive intelligence; Technical intelligence.

See also Compatibility Chart, No.3.

high I.V.	This is only one simple expression of intelligence, signifying a good brain, quick on the uptake, a balanced outlook. Always bear in mind that intelligence is only part of the whole character — graphology paints a holistic picture.
simplification of forms	
speed	
clever connections	
varied	
good spatial layout	
words, sentences and connections pre-eminent over letters and strokes	

Irresponsibility (Also *Insensitivity (to social environment)*)

See also Compatibility Chart, No.14.

neglected writing: missing
  punctuation and parts of words or
  letters
weak stroke
avoidance of the baseline on final
  letters
wavy line/thread connection

Judgement, balanced

See also Compatibility Chart, No.11.

speedy, simplified writing
tapering word size
clever connections
steady base lines
regularity, vertical or right slant
no pastosity

The ability to examine or question a matter using common sense and intelligence, and act upon the result in a reliable manner, free from prejudice and emotional baggage.

Leadership

connectedness
no or few starting strokes
emphasis on last letters
pressure
good sized p.p.'I'
dominant middle zone

Eagerness to exercise leadership. Voluntary acceptance of authority combined with self-confidence and tenacity of purpose.

Loyalty in business

See also Compatibility Chart, No.7.

garlands
leftward tendencies
upward extensions

Strong inclination to bonding, but subject to choice of priorities and the effect of change. Moral perfection is neither on offer nor measurable.

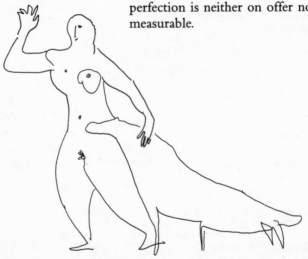

Materialistic ambition

dominant middle zone/lower zone
upward directional tendency
some letters shaped like numerals

A strong desire for affluence.

Maturity

See also Compatibility Chart, No.11.

speedy, simplified writing
tapering word size
clever connections
steady base lines
regularity
upright or rightward slant

Balanced judgement.

Meanness

See also Aloofness. *See also* Compatibility Chart, No.6.

pointed, angular script
narrow word-spacing
absence of end strokes

Meanness, together with harshness,
are attributes of the aloof personality.

Monotony

See Boredom.

Motivating (Also *Training ability*)

angular
rightward tendencies
ascending base lines
pressure
narrow letter-spacing

Conveying knowledge with
enthusiasm. Providing stimuli to
generate interest in targets, ideas,
actions, enterprise.

Organizational ability

clear alignment
regularity
simplification
consistent pressure pattern
zonal balance

Ability to create systematic arrangements for functional co-ordination and interrelation; to economize and simplify work procedures and their presentation.

Originality

See Creative intelligence.

Over-control

angles
arcades
narrow letter-spacing
narrow letter forms
regularity
steady base lines
good alignment, no mingling
no end strokes

Keeping reactions excessively in check.

Perseverance (Also *Tenacity*)

connectedness
angular
steady base lines
pressure
strong 't' bars

Strong persistence; consistent effort; ability to resist side-tracking; steadfast tenacity to completion of task.

Persuasiveness

speed
fluency
angles
pressure
rightward tendency
pronounced capitals

A mixture of reason, enthusiasm and persistence, capable of swaying opinion and gaining acceptance.

Pioneering

rightward slant and tendency
angles
upward line direction
no starting strokes
high, strong 't' bars

Willingness to tackle challenge and competition, and to take risks, mixing courage with a sense of adventure.

Plan-directedness

See Systemic work ability.

Power, need for (Also *Drive*)

rising base line
large overall size
strong 't' bars
firm pressure
strong p.p.'I'
expressive middle zone and lower zone

The urge and ability to take vigorous action to gain control of people, circumstances and affairs.

Problem-solving ability

clear alignment
angles
regularity
simplification
original forms and connections

Clarity; ability to simplify; facility for overcoming or side-stepping (imaginary) obstacles, thus providing a solution to problems.

Productive intelligence

angles
rightward tendencies
legible
balanced zones
regularity

The ability to produce effective solutions to problems.

Punctuality

clear alignment
speed
no starting strokes
wide or widening left margin

Habitually good time-keeping and personal organization in order to meet appointments and deadlines.

Pushiness

angles
connectedness
irregular pressure pattern
upward directional tendency
strong 't' bars and word finals

Using a mixture of chutzpah, aggressiveness, forcefulness and perseverance to achieve aims.

Reliability (Also *Dependability, Honesty*)

See also Compatibility Chart, No.1.

fast, spontaneous, regular, rhythmic
    writing
constant pressure
firm, lively strokes
legible, well-detailed forms with
    diacritics
healthy tension, good balance and
    proportions throughout script

Resilience

balanced zones
regularity
rhythm
steady base lines
flexible slant

Ability to take in one's stride
setbacks, opposition, criticism,
pressure, periods of stress.

Resourcefulness

See Ingenuity.

Responsibility (Also *Caring; Concern for others*)

See also Compatibility Chart, No.13.

protective indications such as
   'roofing' — 't' bars or capital
   endings spanning the whole word
angles
consistent pressure pattern
good size upper zone
regularity
legibility
conventional types: some arcades

Reliability, integrity, sense of duty and
care, personal identification and
feelings of involvement.

Result-orientated

angles
vertical or right slant
good size middle zone/lower zone
steady base lines
regular
no starting strokes

Goal-directed, concerned with
minimizing money, time and energy
expended; confident of own abilities;
not shy of accepting commission as
(part) payment.

Risk-taking

sizeable middle zone
disconnectedness
varying directional tendencies
strong signature

Possessing good judgement, self-
confidence and decision-making ability,
sense of adventure and the capacity
to deal with changing fortunes,
commercial gain or loss.

Rule-following

various forms of connection
no last letter emphasis/threads
moderate middle zone
moderate p.p.'I'

Disposed to follow rules and
procedures with comfort;
yielding to instructions and
directions; obedience and respect for
superiors; a sense of responsibility.

Sales ability

ascending base lines
no starting strokes
rightward tendencies
expressive freedom
left margin wide or widening
decisive word finals
irregularity

The ability to discover hitherto virgin
territory; to find new angles of
approach — outsmarting the
competition— and to sell profitably to
resistant buyers; tuning in to customers'
needs, and knowing when and how to
close a sale.

Sales management ability

angles
simplification
connectedness
zonal balance
sizeable capitals and p.p.'I'
rhythmic use of space

Ability to direct, plan and organize,
motivate, co-ordinate, control and
administer the total sales effort or
sales force.

Self-assurance

See also Confident self-presentation.

rhythm
no excesses
consistent pressure pattern
normal size and form of p.p.'I'

A feeling of comfort within oneself, a
prerequisite of self-confidence.

Self-confidence

See also Confident self-presentation.

sizeable middle zone
capitals not excessive
p.p.'I' in line with the rest of the script
normal size
regularity
flexible forms and connections

A positive appreciation of own abilities.

Self-control

angles
narrow letter-spacing
regularity
steady base lines
good alignment, no mingling

Being able to keep one's reactions in check. Over-control is indicated when one or more of the features appears in excess in the script.

Selfishness

See also Compatibility Chart, No.8.

leftward tendencies
claw-like leftward tendencies
slow, inhibited writing
irregular/illegible
exaggerations in size and width

Sense of humour

See Friendliness; Imagination.

Sincerity

quick, clear, spontaneous
rhythmic, readable, lively
no closing of vowels or touching up

Sociability

garlands
right slant
various forms of connection
normal p.p.'I'
well but not over-rounded

Disposed toward friendly interaction with different groups and types of people; being able to tolerate a variety of opinions.

Stability

steady base lines
rhythm
spatial alignment
zonal regularity
consistent pressure pattern

Having resolution of purpose and steadfastness based on emotional balance.

Stupidity

See also Compatibility Chart, No.4.

slow
copybook writing
irregular and awkward forms
lack of individuality
lack of spatial awareness

Systematic work ability (Also *Plan-directedness*)

angles
simplification
no starting strokes
zonal balance
decisive word finals

Capable of focusing on the realization of plans; able to absorb and evaluate information; to translate into a methodical sequence of activities the various aspects of a situation or task; able to set priorities to realize tasks within available time.

Tact, diplomacy

garlands, threads
light pressure
rising baseline
subtle variety
small writing

Team spirit

no starting strokes
rightward tendencies
no first letter emphasis
garlands/thread connections
normal p.p.'I'

The ability to act, work and co-operate
with others for a common purpose
and without claims to leadership and
domination.

Technical intelligence and creativity

regular middle zone
angles
pressure
connectedness
drawn or individualized letter forms
no starting strokes

Technical inventiveness relating to
practical design. The ability to
function effectively in technical
matters, applying the findings,
procedures and principles of systematic
investigation into the identification of
problems and their creative solution.

Tenacity

See Perseverance.

Unreliability

See Dishonesty. *See also* Compatibility Chart, No.2.

Urge to win

angles
arcades
vertical or left slant
strong or dominant middle zone
dominant lower zone
strong p.p.'I'
strong signature

The compulsion to come out on top; the subconscious drive to gain victory for self-gratification, rather than competitive excellence.

Vitality

See Energy.

Analysis per job

The handwriting analyst often receives the barest minimum of detail from the client company. He will summarize these, then define the general job requirements and the aptitude and skills needed with the help of an I.T. Chart. See the following example.

The client

Large electronics and engineering company which researches, designs and produces advanced apparatus and systems for the UK Ministry of Defence. Multi-million pound sterling contracts involving several years of work require dedicated personnel in the computer programming section, where all employees are security vetted. Secrecy and stability are of further importance because a number of people working on the project have met with fatal accidents, disappeared or committed inexplicable suicide.

General job requirements	*Aptitude, skills needed*
computer skills	fluency in writing
	accuracy in detail
	analytical intelligence
	systematic, methodical, organizational skills

Special requirements	
to support security vetting	balanced, reserved, alert, reliable
self-starter	initiative, resourceful
ability to work with little supervision	independence, discrimination (i.e. ability to make precise judgements) self-confidence
constant worker, keen to carry out and deal with all aspects of the job, monotonous as well as interesting	commitment to duty, result/goal-orientated
long, irregular hours if need be	perseverance, stamina
isolated, sedentary work	loner, at ease with own company, limited need for social contacts
ability to keep calm	pressure/frustration tolerance
Note: for medical check-up	good eyesight
	not colour blind
	no back/neck injuries
	not prone to migraine/headaches

The I.T. Chart: an integral system applied to functions and tasks in information technology

	SYSTEM DEVELOPMENT					SUPPORT								
FUNCTION TASKS	Project leader and advisor	Information analyst	System designer	Applications programmer	Techno-scientific analyst/programmer	IT Coordinator and advisor	OA Support analyst	PC Support counsellor	IT Training advisor	Internal auditor and data security advisor	Database administrator	Procedures analyst	Hardware and system software counsellor	Librarian
APTITUDE SKILLS	SD1	SD2	SD3	SD4	SD5	SUP1	SUP2	SUP3	SUP4	SUP5	SUP6	SUP7	SUP8	SUP9
Communication skills. Fluency: verbal and written	•	•	•	+	+	•	•	+	•	•	+	•	•	−
Motivation and training ability. Enthusiasm	•	+	+	+	+	•	•	•	•	•	+	•	+	−
Decisiveness	•	+	+	−	+	•	+	+	+	+	+	+	•	+
Accuracy in detail	+	•	•	•	•	+	+	•	+	•	−	+	+	•
Sociability, commitment, empathy	•	•	+	+	+	•	•	•	•	+	+	+	•	+
Cooperative team spirit	•	•	•	+	+	•	+	+	+	+	+	+	+	+
Power of persuasion. Negotiating skills	•	•	•	−	+	•	•	−	•	•	•	+	+	−
Analytical intelligence. Problem-solving ability	•	•	•	+	•	•	+	+	+	+	+	•	•	+
Resourcefulness and creativity	•	•	•	+	•	•	+	+	+	+	+	+	•	−
Systematic, methodical, organizational ability	•	•	•	•	•	•	+	+	+	•	•	•	•	•
Stamina, perseverance	•	•	•	•	+	•	+	+	+	•	+	+	+	−
Pressure resistance. Frustration tolerance	•	−	−	−	−	•	+	−	+	+	•	+	+	−
• Very important	11	9	8	3	4	11	4	3	4	6	3	4	6	2
+ Quite important	1	2	3	6	7	1	8	7	8	6	8	8	6	4
− Less important	0	1	1	3	1	0	0	2	0	0	1	0	0	6

IT= Information Technology

OA= Office Automation

APTITUDE SKILLS / FUNCTION TASKS	APPLICATION								COORDINATION DECENTRALIZED SYSTEM APPLICATION			
	System software programmer	Network specialist	Production and problem analyst	Production controller	Capacity controller	Helpdesk customer service staff member	Chief operator	Network operator	Coordinator (IT)	Data manager	Application manager	Coordination system controller
	AP1	AP2	AP3	AP4	AP5	AP6	AP7	AP8	CO1	CO2	CO3	CO4
Communication skills Fluency: verbal and written	+	+	•	• / −		•	+	−	•	•	•	+
Motivation and training ability. Enthusiasm	−	−	•	+ / −		•	+	−	•	•	+	
Decisiveness	+	+	•	+	+	+	•	−	•	•	•	−
Accuracy in detail	•	•	•	•	•	+	•	•	+	•	•	+
Sociability, commitment, empathy	−	+	•	•	−	•	•	−	•	•	•	+
Cooperative team spirit	+	+	+	•	−	•	•	+	•	•	•	+
Power of persuasion Negotiating skills	−	−	•	•	−	•	+	−	•	•	+	−
Analytical intelligence Problem-solving ability	•	•	•	+	+	+	−	−	•	•	+	−
Resourcefulness and creativity	•	•	•	•	+	•	+	+	•	•	+	+
Systematic, methodical, organizational ability	•	•	•	+	•	•	•	•	•	•	+	•
Stamina, perseverance	•	•	•	•	−	•	+	+	•	•	+	+
Pressure resistance Frustration tolerance	−	−	+	+	−	+	+	−	•	+	−	−
• Very important	5	5	10	6	2	8	5	2	11	11	5	1
+ Quite important	3	4	2	5	3	4	6	3	1	1	6	6
− Less important	4	2	0	0	7	0	1	7	0	0	1	5

IT= Information Technology
OA= Office Automation

Compatibility in business, the professions and personal relationships

Good partnerships are based not only on compatibility of character but on factors outside the analyst's assessment: events, circumstances, sympathies, subjective elements and peculiarities of others involved. In a business relationship, such as a partnership or a manager or director and his or her personal assistant, it is advisable to have both scripts analysed. An analyst will be able to pinpoint areas of likely antagonism or hostility, and features that are likely to harmonize.

It is possible, however, to offer guidelines you can use to judge the probable compatibility or otherwise of yourself and a potential partner or personal assistant. In the left-hand column below are listed the qualities most often required of close associates — honesty, intelligence, friendliness and so on. In the right-hand column are listed their contrasting

qualities — the negative personality features you are least likely to want to have to work with.

To use the chart, first list the feature(s) you consider most important — and those you consider least desirable. Next, turn to Psychological Clusters (Appendix 2), and search through the alphabetical list of character traits for the feature(s) you have listed. Clustered under each heading is a number of handwriting features that indicate that handwriting trait.

For example, if No. 13 on the list below ('Caring, consideration and concern for others, sense of responsibility') are qualities you consider important in your partner, turn to the Psychological Clusters section and look them up. You will find a number of handwriting features listed under 'Caring' and 'Responsibility'. These are the features which should be expected in your applicants' handwriting samples. However, never forget: let the writing speak to you, and not the other way around. Pages 150–1 also list handwriting features under 'Insensitivity' and 'Irresponsibility'. Clearly, should you be seriously considering any applicant whose handwriting sample indicates any of these features, it would be sensible to send the sample for expert analysis. To be ruled by prudence and foresight at this stage of the selection process could save you from the stress of a difficult working relationship — and wasted financial resources — in the future.

Compatibility Chart
Important compatibility qualities, positive and negative

1. **Honesty**
   reliability
   dependability

2. **Dishonesty**
   lack of reliability
   lack of dependability
   lying

3. **Intelligence**

4. **Stupidity**

5. **Friendliness**
   generosity
   empathy

6. **Aloofness**
   harshness
   meanness
   brutality

7. **Altruism**
   integrity
   loyalty to colleagues

8. **Selfishness**
   lack of principle
   disloyalty

9. **Adaptability**
   willingness to listen
   cooperativeness

10. **Inflexibility**
   dogmatism
   discordance
   lack of cooperative
   spirit

11. **Maturity**
   balanced judgement

12. **Immaturity**
   lack of experience
   indecision
   bad judgement

13. **Caring, consideration
   and concern for others**
   sense of responsibility

14. **Uncaring**
   thoughtless
   egocentric
   irresponsible
   insensitivity to
      social environment

15. **Openness**
   straightforwardness
   sincerity

16. **Posing**
   pretending
   hiding
   lying
   misleading
   being double-faced

17. **Imagination**
   sense of humour

18. **Boredom**
   dull
   unadventurous

Appendix 5

Career pointers

These career parters show what the function entails for career choice and guidance, use in advertising, job specifications and interview check lists.

Accountant (qualified)

(mainly sedentary and confined to work area)
Analytical; quick grasp of essential facts involving figures; attentive to detail; insight; perceptive; precise; good concentration; independent; patient; objective; resistant to pressure; able to advise; able to work with clients; leadership qualities; controlled; reserved; high ethical standards; open, enquiring mind, capable of clarity; stable.

Accountant (trainee)

(must be prepared for low pay and long hours while training)
Intelligent; well educated; quick with figures; computer-literate; able to spot trends from details; sense of presentation and order; ability to budget and to project ahead; able to work alone and in a team; perseverance.

Pressure-resistant

Administrator, general

Dependable; attentive to detail; pride in work; organized; patient; good memory; good with people; flexible; compliant; resistant to pressure and frustration; computer-literate. *See also* **Hospital manager**.

Advertising account executive

Enthusiastic; people skills; engaging; creative; clarifying; motivating; good communicator; self-starter; solo and team worker; selling ability.

Architect

Strong visual sense; sensitive to form, line and colour; creative thinker; imaginative; practical; numerate; attentive to detail; highly responsible; goal-oriented; flexible; feel for the politics of the attainable; co-operative; leadership qualities; good coordinator; facility for self expression through drawing, writing and verbal communication.

Artist, commercial

Good sense of form, line and colour; patient; original; manual dexterity; able to empathize; grasp of the essential; able to prioritize.

Banker

Imagination and empathy mixed with caution; team leader; balanced; adaptable; self-esteem; integrity; attentive to detail; mathematical and analytical ability; dignity; diplomatic; common sense; initiative; organizing ability; intelligence; sales and people skills; objectivity; ambition; output- and result-directed; able to assimilate technical knowledge rapidly; decisive.

**Banker,
personal**

(sales skills are important in this job; *see* **Sales representative**)

Able to identify suitable marketing opportunities; able to assimilate diverse product knowledge; able to adjust to change and expansion; helpful and courteous attitude towards customers, not too pushy, but intent on closing deals.

**Banking,
counter staff**

Good appearance; client-orientated; helpful manner and attitude; pride in work; fast; accurate; alert; teamworker; reliable; honest; able to absorb criticism.

**Banking,
international
services officer**

(job requires financial sophistication)
Intelligent; organized; linguist; good communicator; teamworker; able to assimilate and put into practice the technical knowledge required for the finance of international trade and international banking services; efficient; good with people from other cultures and clients with international requirements.

Barrister

Independent; assertive; diplomatic; good communicator; intelligent; logical; integrity; keen perception; innovative; quick-witted; stamina; able to work alone; concentration; thoroughness; competitive; able to cope with heavy workload in limited time.

**Building,
contractor**

Good organizer, team-builder; negotiator; confident calculator; decisive; attentive to detail; precise; resourceful; flexible; technically competent; pride in standard of work and delivery in time.

Building, quantity surveyor

Able to work with technical detail; able to think and take decisions 'on the hoof'; logical; numerate; foresight; good organizer; practical; resourceful; responsible; flexible; proactive; thorough; negotiator skills; pride in good progress and time-keeping; teamworker; stamina; resistant to pressure and frustration.

Buyer

Intelligent; integrity; linguist; good with figures; good with people; imaginative; attentive to detail; planning ability; intuitive; decisive; responsible; stamina; resistance to jet-lag (for long-distance travel).

Careers/ employment counsellor

Analytical; adaptable; objective; aptitude for clerical work; articulate; good listener; stamina; patient; determined; persistent; will-power; research ability; organized; enthusiastic; attentive to detail; empathy; altruistic; co-operative; able to implement policy correctly.

Chauffeur/ driver, company

(job involves client contact and confidential or money-collecting duties)

Good appearance; pride in the appearance of his or her vehicle; common sense; manual dexterity; honest; punctual; compliant; dependable; stamina; patient; resistant to stress caused by traffic.

Chef

(required to work anti-social hours)

Creative; good organizer; management ability; drive; energetic; a motivator; able to supervise; attentive to detail; decisive; independent thinker; intuitive; consumer-sensitive; artistic ability; clean; practical.

Civil servant

Able to take orders; tolerant of routine; persistent; integrity; pride; dignity; loyalty; stamina; attentive to detail; objective; willing to implement policy correctly; able to withstand hostility; teamworker; good with people; pride in professionalism; discreet.

Computer programmer

Clear, logical thinker; consistent; stamina; analytical; patient; proud; loyal; persistent; accurate; abstract imagination; goal-directed; tenacious; able to work under pressure.

Designer, industrial

A designer has to be: creative; able to synthesize, combine different technologies within the body of one machine (a simple example is a computer manipulated lathe, or an assembly line with different robotics and incoming supplies to build part of a car.) A designer must understand what the market requires now (shape, colour, design) and in the near future (so that retooling is not necessary). A designer must be cost-conscious, relating, for example, space, weight and quality allowed, required or desirable, to achievable price, profit objective and market segment. A designer must therefore have an empathy with sales, in order to produce saleable designs.

Engineer/ technical workshop manager

Leadership qualities; responsible; communicative; a motivator; practical; manual dexterity; logical; mathematical ability; precise; good concentration; attentive to detail; methodical; analytical and planning ability; able to organize; stamina; perseverance; takes pride in output; able to manage material and human resources.

Exchange dealer

Responsible; quick-thinking; good concentration; computer-literate; highly stress-resistant; emotionally stable; decisive (but not impulsive); analytical; opportunistic.

Farm manager — Good organizer; business acumen; decisive; a 'doer'; short- and long-term planning ability; empathy with nature; mental and physical stamina; good health; technical understanding; knowledge of administration and budgeting; a motivator; liking for outdoor work; responsibility; emotional balance.

Financial advisor — (job requires sophistication in financial matters) Client-oriented; integrity; initiative; planning ability; attentive to detail; good communicator; patient; persevering.

Handwriting analyst/ graphologist — Analytical ability; open-mindedness; problem-solver; knowledge of and insight into psychology; interest in people; verbal and written fluency; determined; organized; tactful; perceptive; able to weigh and evaluate a variety of often contrasting details and construct a guiding image from them; objective.

Hospital manager — Organized; attentive to detail; analytical ability; diplomatic; tactful; perceptive; cautious; patient; initiative; determined; decisive; self-reliant; sensitive to economic and legal considerations; articulate; resistant to pressure and frustration.

Hotel manager — (job involves long, anti-social hours) Team leader; good with people; good organizer; outgoing personality; tactful; firm; good communicator; able to deal with the public; decisive; stamina; good delegator; good supervisor; motivated to deal instantly with a variety of tasks and problems; detailed knowledge of functions under his or her responsibility.

Insurance executive — Financial, planning and selling abilities; long-term perspective; good with people; confident self-presentation; good communicator; administrative and reporting skills; integrity; tact.

Insurance loss adjustor — Problem-solver; project-oriented; attentive to detail; tough; good negotiator; self-reliant; integrity; good administrator, reporting skills.

Manager, general — Leadership qualities; able to develop policies that stretch, integrate and propel company activities; insight; self-confidence; sound judgment in weighing up past experience and diverse information in order to make decisions; able to reconcile conflicting interests; awareness of management role, power and responsibility.

See also **Farm manager; Hospital manager; Hotel manager; Office manager; Personnel manager; Project manager; Sports manager; Theatre manager**.

Medical practitioner

(anti-social hours)
Intelligence; analytical; intuitive; empathy; approachable; good memory for people and facts; open-minded; stress-resistant; courageous; supportive; knowledge of planning, administration and budgeting; a motivator; team leader; physical and mental stamina; good listener; comforting; confident manner; takes pride in prevention of illness, quick diagnosis and healthy results.

Good listener

Office manager

Self-confident; good organizer; able to work alone and in a team; clear self-expression; tidy; accurate; methodical; good memory; firm yet tactful; resourceful; problem-solver; good communicator; pride in efficiency; able to maintain a good atmosphere under pressure.

Personnel manager

People skills; willing to implement policy correctly; administrative ability; altruistic; tactful; tough; objective; balanced; self-confident; responsible; good communicator; teamworker; able to take and give instructions.

Project manager

Able to supervise or exercise authority over the execution of projects or technologically complex tasks involving detailed specifications and objectives within limited time and budget. Able to evaluate and organize staff; able to lead, direct, supervise or decide; able to plan, control and guide a project from inception to completion.

Psychologist

(must be prepared to avoid exercising power over patients, bonding, and submission)
Perception; intuition; good comprehension; objective; analytical ability; integrity; diplomatic; articulate; good listener; able to handle stress; patient; result-orientated.

Psychotherapist

Intelligent; problem-solver; able to differentiate between fact and fantasy, perception and reality; empathy with people; patience; able to work independently with concepts and intangibles.

Publishing, commissioning editor

Analytical and critical abilities; a combination of creativity, imagination and intuition with commercial judgement and a good visual sense; able to work independently and to convey ideas to others enthusiastically; tact and sensitivity; able to keep several balls in the air at once; diplomacy; dedication.

Publishing, desk editor

High level of literacy; accuracy; good concentration; computer skills; able to work independently; objectivity; empathy, tact; common sense; meticulous eye for, and love of, detail, combined with the ability to distinguish the wood from the trees.

Publishing, production manager

Negotiating skills, efficiency; calm under pressure; good at prioritizing; fast-thinking; accuracy with financial data; able to delegate.

Sales representative

(must be able to create exactly the right immediate impression; support, back-up, bonding and signs of appreciation may well increase success rate)
Self-starter; quick thinker; articulate; self-confident; outward and goal-directed; determined; persistent; proactive and reactive; intuitive; good memory; love of variety, change and challenge; pride in closing a deal; competitive spirit; money-minded; opportunistic; achiever.

Secretary, senior/personal assistant, professional practice manager/ess

(occasional or regular overtime and anti-social hours)
Good appearance; cheerful; well-spoken, with a clear voice and an engaging telephone manner; discreet; intelligence; tact; initiative; able to communicate at all levels; methodical; punctual; quick-witted; versatile; flexible, but not a push-over; good organizer; written and verbal reporting skills; filing skills; interested in people; computer-literate; high degree of literacy; numerate; accurate; good memory; reliable; common sense.

Self-employed person

Ambitious; initiative, pride in achievement; self-confident; self-esteem; self-motivation; self-discipline; administrative and organizational ability; tolerant of routine; determined; persistent; stamina; good memory; flexible; good with people; willingness to tackle a variety of tasks and to work long hours; opportunistic in a positive sense.

Planning ability

Social worker   Emotionally stable; mature; objective; self-confident; independent; attentive to detail; diplomatic; co-operative; open-minded; warm personality; intuitive; investigative; good judgement; enthusiastic; dispassionate.

Solicitor   Intelligence; integrity; empathy; able to assimilate knowledge quickly and thoroughly; good listener; clear communicator; able to work with others; good delegator; attentive to detail; penetrating insight; able to see things through; stamina; resistant to pressure; neat; organized; independent.

Sports manager   (manager of sports professionals)
Management ability; good organizer; financial skills; good negotiator; physical and mental stamina; talented; persistent; strong will-power; self-disciplined; enthusiastic; achiever; team player with solo qualities; initiative; determined; precise; courageous; competitive.

Teacher/trainer   (a job requiring vocational calling – able to take pride in students' results)
Authority; enthusiastic; verbal and written fluency; alert; observant; analytical; objective; patient; open-minded; adaptable; energetic; stamina; administrative and reporting ability; good communicator; consistent; encouraging – a motivator; approachable; reliable; capacity for self-criticism; organized; punctual; optimistic; pragmatic.

Theatre manager   People and organizational skills; planning, administrative and budgeting ability; good health; creative; innovative; imaginative; assertive; good with people; problem-solver – resourceful in emergencies; pressure-proof.

Appendix 6

Honesty/risk chart

Caution: Some of the following trends can be observed at times in almost any handwriting. Only if at least four or five indications reappear frequently in the same script should you contemplate a conclusion of possible dishonesty, of *risk*.

Let us assume you have three candidates: X, Y and Z. They all have a high I.V. with mature script. You mark square 2 under *Above Average* for X, Y and Z. Let us now take a look at the baseline, square 10. Say you allocate X to *Above Average*, Y to *Good Average*, Z to *Fair*. Next, in say square 14, Balanced p.p.'I', you allocate X to *Above Average*, Y to *Fair*, Z to *Below Average*. When you have worked your way through the list, add the totals for X, Y and Z. You can then determine whether any of them must be regarded as a risk. In such a case, you are advised to recheck the c.v., references, etc. with utmost care, if there is no alternative choice, otherwise to continue your search for a more suitable candidate.

You may copy this chart and add it to your check list.

The Honesty/Risk Chart

	Above Average	Good Medium Average	Fair Below Average	Below Average	Area of Risk
1. Fast writing.					Slow writing.
2. High I.V., mature script.					Artificial, immature script.
3. Clear, legible script.					Unnecessary retouching (not improving legibility).
4. Distinctive letterforms.					Letters looking like other letters.
5. Free movement.					Initial emphasis, frequent interruption, many letters inserted.
6. Clear ovals.					Letter ovals of 'a', 'b', 'd', 'g', 'o', 'q' open at the base, with LT. Looped ovals.
7. Capitals in balance with the rest of the writing.					Disproportionate sized capitals. Uneven MZ letters, jutting out.
8. Clear of excessive dots.					Excess dots, punctuation, resting points.
9. Letterforms consistent.					Fragmented letters, parts missing, combined with slowness in mature script.
10. Even baseline.					Erratic baseline, script shows lability and threads.
11. Rightward tendencies.					Strong leftward tendencies.
12. Clear stroke quality.					Slack, muddy strokes.
13. Pressure consistency.					Displaced pressure.
14. Balanced p.p.'I'.					Malformed or small p.p.'I'.
Totals					
	X,Y,Z	X,Y,Z	X,Y,Z	X,Y,Z	

Appendix 7

Graphological reports

In this section graphological reports on three well known figures are followed by three anonymous reports. As well as being of interest to graphologists, these also provide a means of testing the reader's own analytical ability.

The following chart shows what is meant by 'good intelligence' or 'fair average' in the reports. Fifty per cent of the population is graded as 'average'.

IQ	± %	Approximate IQ distribution
		dazzling! (in a way)
+ 140	2%	exceptionally intelligent
130	7%	highly intelligent
120	17%	good intelligence, bright
110	25%	good average
100		AVERAGE of the population
90	25%	fair average
80	17%	below average
70	7%	well below average
− 60	2%	mentally underprivileged

Margaret Thatcher

Clear, with remarkable spatial quality; good black/white balance; aerated: independent; keen judgement.

Rhythmic: controlled will-power.

Vertical slant: will-power; faithful to personal ethics; need for freedom.

High 't' bars: self-control; social ambition.

Large distance between words: need for clarity, overview.

Pastosity: warmth of feeling.

Small script with large capitals: desire to lead; need for recognition.

Intelligence and personality

The personality level of this writer is very good and her handwriting indicates a high intelligence.

She possesses an analytical mind and a sharp critical sense.

She is a clear strategic thinker with the ability to get quickly to the heart of a matter and to discern which issues are relevant and which are not. She is able to concentrate on essentials.

The handwriting shows excellent mental equipment — the writer has the ability to absorb ideas and translate them into functional operations. She can think things through in a step-by-step manner, but also has the benefit of intuition.

Attitude towards work

This writer is a dynamic, result-oriented woman, who proceeds with steady energy in the accomplishment of her tasks. She is hard-working and determined in her efforts to succeed. She has a strong sense of purpose and gets things done promptly and without hesitation.

She doesn't panic in times of crisis, is goal-oriented, can make up her mind and take action. She is generally optimistic and hard to discourage.

This writer is an independent woman who has a clear view of where she is heading. She values her freedom highly and finds it hard to follow the dictates of others. She is a good, clever organizer, with an eye to the future and a good sense

10 DOWNING STREET

13th June 1987

Dear Mrs.

The result of this election has been both a historic achievement for our Party and a confirmation of the soundness of our policies.

Thank you for everything you did to make our local campaign such a success. We have never had a better organisation — and the spirit was truly wonderful.

Yours sincerely

Margaret Thatcher

of arrangement. Although decisive, she does not make up her mind hastily on matters of importance.

This writer is capable of handling varied and diversified tasks and she often immediately sees the consequences of alternative lines of action.

Attitude towards others

This writer is presentable and understands the importance of creating a good image. She is well-mannered and correct in her behaviour towards others.

She can communicate her ideas lucidly and is able to impose her will. She can inspire confidence in others.

The writer is quite a determined woman and faithful to her personal ethics. She has decided opinions and she speaks her mind. She clearly has the courage of her convictions and if she believes her own ideas are right she will show a strong determination to get her own way. However, although decisive, she usually respects another's opinion and as a rule she is prepared to discuss and to listen to others. Her handwriting shows a desire to lead and a need for recognition, but she is not insensitive to the feelings of others. As a rule, she acts in a tactful manner and takes account of other people's needs. She is often able to say the right thing at the right time.

The handwriting show richness of feeling; the writer is basically a warm sort of person. She is receptive, but in a framework of control.

John Major

Dominant in this script: narrowness.

Narrowness and regularity and angles: self-control; concentration; inner strength.

Narrowness and evenness: self-confidence.

Angles and great differences in length: ambition; competitive spirit.

Strong pressure, compact writing: strength.

Horizontal pressure on 't' bars: obstinacy.

Down-slanted 't' bars: a fighter.

1O DOWNING STREET
LONDON SW1A 2AA

Thank you so much for your kind message of congratulation. Such support is heart warming especially in view of all the hard work that lies ahead.

With that historic fourth victory behind us, we can press ahead with building economic recovery and extending choice and opportunity ever more widely. With the backing of so very many people, I am confident that those great prizes are within our reach.

It was kind of you to write.

Yours sincerely,

John Major

The signature

High upper zone letters in the signature indicate a man with ideas; the probing lower zone shows that they are well rooted. The pressure and narrowness of the script shows drive and ambition; a tough, disciplined worker. The strong lines, compact middle zone, the 'j' dot near the stem and the upright slant of the 'n' in 'John' point to strong perseverance, clarity and realism.

The open final letters show just that: receptivity, a willingness to listen, a reaching towards the future. The bulk of the signature shows, however, that ultimately the writer will make up his own mind and stand for it. While outwardly willing to listen, if he thinks he is right he will not let anyone interfere with his plans and ideas. He is not as open as he may seem, and where his deeper feelings are concerned, he keeps others at a distance. He gives away nothing of importance about himself.

A good man to have as a friend. Reliable.

Intelligence and personality

The personality level of this writer is of a good average and his handwriting indicates good intelligence.

He has a sharp mind and he is a clear strategic thinker.

His handwriting shows a direct and penetrating thought process and a well-developed critical sense. The writer has sound reasoning and the ability to recognize cause and effect.

He is not really original in his approach, but being logical, analytical and realistic, he is capable of reaching practical solutions.

Attitude towards work

This writer is a hard worker and determined in his efforts to succeed. He is a fighter who enjoys achieving goals in the face of obstacles. He wants to win and can be aggressive in tackling problems. He is resolute and has strong drive. He is tenacious and doesn't panic in times of crisis. He puts his mind to the job and goes after his objective in a direct, focused manner. As a rule, he sets realistic goals and he knows exactly what he wants to achieve.

The writer is a competitive, ambitious and goal-oriented individual. He has independence of attitude, is capable of acting on his own and is ready to rely on himself. He is strong-willed and inclined to go about things his own way. He is very persistent, which may occasionally lead to a lack of flexibility. He can reject authority and finds it hard to follow the dictates of others.

This man's organizational skills are well developed. He can develop and agree short, mid and long-term objectives. His problem-solving is not always innovative, but it is likely to be positive and thorough. The handwriting shows a perceptiveness about practical matters.

The way of acting of this writer is deliberate. He is systematic, precise and logical. He takes time to plan through complex matters, rather than tackling what is immediately obvious. Although decisive, he usually shows care and restraint in his actions and decisions over important matters.

Attitude towards others

This writer is personable and understands the importance of creating a good image. He is presentable and correct in his behaviour towards others.

He is a self-confident person and his handwriting shows inner strength. He is able to impose his will and inspire confidence in others. He is a leader, ready to take charge and to make decisions.

Although at first sight he seems friendly and easy-going, his handwriting shows strength of will that rarely permits compromise. Outwardly he is willing to listen to people, but once he has made up his mind, he is insistent and won't take no for an answer. He is capable of standing up to resistance from others and of sticking to something he believes in, even if it is unpopular. If he thinks he is right he will not let anyone interfere with his plans and ideas.

In his behaviour towards others this writer can make an open impression, but he is fairly tight-lipped where his deeper feelings are concerned. Despite talkativeness, he gives away nothing of any importance about himself and he is quite good at hiding his feelings from others. Inner control blocks his spontaneity and he doesn't want to allow himself to be known too well by the outside world.

Cliff Richard

Author's note: Nigel Cutteridge, a freelance producer, composed a programme with Mandy Wheeler Sound Productions for BBC Radio 2 to celebrate Cliff Richard's 50th birthday. After analysing the writing of the 'mystery male', during the interview I said, 'It could be someone like Cliff Richard . . .'

High I.V., looks good, well proportioned; precise strokes: direct, penetrating.

Disconnected writing and angles: critical ability.

High loops in 'h' and 't' bar above middle zone: idealistic.

Lower zone accent in 'f': realistic.

Pastosity: imagination, warmth.

Second downstroke of 'n' rounded: empathy; consideration for others.

Angles and left slant on 'y', 'g': will not mince his words.

Alternating left-right slant: need for contact *and* distance.

Intelligence and personality

The personality level of this writer is good and his handwriting indicates a good intelligence.

The writer has critical ability and is able to judge independently. He has a penetrating and direct thought process. The handwriting shows a combination of quick mental recall, sound reasoning and the ability to recognize cause and effect.

There is a richness of ideas here and a vivid, but controlled imagination. Despite mental versatility and adaptability, he can think systematically through problems and tasks from start to finish. This man's intuition is usually reliable.

Hi - it's great to be back with you and thanks for turning out to watch the show. With every passing year it gets more difficult to ring the changes. In '89 we staged "the Event", a massive extravaganza at London's Wembley Stadium - Some of you might have seen it on T.V. Last year I performed part of it for you & it left me wondering what I could do as a follow-up. More dancers? More musicians? More moving lights? Bigger effects? In the end I decided <u>none</u> of those things.

Tonight you've got just me & my guitar & a few friends & it's going to give me the chance to sing for you, songs I haven't performed for years! It's the first time we've used this kind of format & I hope you enjoy it."

Luv

Cliff.

The handwriting shows idealistic tendencies, but he rarely gets carried away. As a rule, he is level-headed and faces reality with a clear mind.

Attitude towards work

This writer is a result-oriented individual who usually has a clear idea of where he is heading. He is a hard worker and determined in his effort to succeed. For the most part he is tenacious. He can handle disappointments: he recovers quickly and starts anew. He doesn't panic easily.

This writer is an independent man who likes to be able to make his own decisions and to get on with the job. He doesn't like to be tied down and needs variety in his work. He is full of ideas and in the main can implement them. He is well organized and usually systematic and precise in his work.

Attitude towards others

As a rule this writer uses tact and diplomacy in his dealings with others and he takes account of other people's feelings and needs. However, he is not as easy-going as he may seem at first. Once he has made up his mind he is rather insistent and determined not to let anybody interfere with his plans and ideas.

He speaks his mind when necessary and if he thinks he is right he will not mince his words. He is sufficiently receptive of the ideas of others, but he has the courage of his own convictions.

This writer appears to be an extrovert, but he is not quite as spontaneous as his outer behaviour might imply. He is a warm sort of person, but where his deeper feelings are concerned he initially keeps people at a safe distance. On the one hand he has a need for close contact, on the other he is a very private person.

Report No.1 *Female, 32. Administrator.*

As soon as I left university I started working as a freelance independent video maker, mostly for community groups and government funded bodies. Over a period of six years I made a number of productions

Left margin fluctuating: inner ambivalence.

Leftward slant: afraid of getting involved; inner control; introversive.

Pastosity: warmth of feeling.

Fluctuations in letter size, MZ: fluctuating self-esteem.

Long 't' bars, often slanted down: defensive, irritable.

Intelligence and personality

The personality level of this writer is above average and her handwriting indicates a good intelligence.

Her intellect is sharply observing and clarifying and she can see the relationships of parts within the whole of situations and structures. Her handwriting shows a penetrating and direct thought process. She is able to get to the heart of a matter and to discern which issues are relevant and which are not.

Through a combination of common sense, logic and receptivity, this writer is capable of reaching practical solutions.

Attitude towards work

This writer has a slight tendency to inner ambivalence. Mood swings influence her behaviour at times; however, as a rule she is able to exercise self-control and once she decides to do something she is a well-disciplined worker.

She is not dynamic by nature and her capacity to tolerate extended stress is doubtful. On the whole, however, she is a fairly consistent worker and when handling familiar tasks she is able to keep calm and collected most of the time.

This writer can work independently and likes to be able to complete a job on her own. She can handle her own responsibility. She may find it hard to fit into structured and rigid frameworks.

Her organizational skills are well developed. She can plan and schedule work and pays attention to detail. Her way of acting is well considered.

The writer has the ability to concentrate on her work and to ignore intrusions.

Attitude towards others

This writer has good communication skills and she is able to find the right tone in her behaviour towards others. As a rule she acts in a tactful manner and doesn't antagonize others intentionally.

She can communicate her ideas lucidly and she is able to convey knowledge and experience to others. She is a good adviser and able to listen. She can absorb and use what she hears.

This writer presents herself skilfully and usually gives the impression of being well in control. However, she is not as sure of herself as she portrays. Her self-esteem fluctuates between confidence on the one hand and insecurity on the other. The insecurity may cause her to be defensive on occasion and slightly irritable if she is unable to implement her ideas. For the most part, however, she can exercise self-control and she is likely to communicate in a diplomatic manner.

This writer is basically a warm sort of person, but afraid of really getting involved. Inner control blocks her spontaneity and despite talkativeness she gives away nothing of importance about herself. She thinks before she speaks and where her deeper feelings are concerned she likes to keep others at a safe distance. This writer relates to others pleasantly but somewhat superficially. She usually appears extrovert, but in reality she is an introversive person giving the impression of outwardness. She dislikes people intruding into her privacy.

Report No.2   *Male, 40-ish. Accountant.*

Author's note: This initial sceptic confessed that the report was 'extraordinarily accurate in the generality', adding, 'whilst in respect of certain characteristics I am quite unable to understand how you deduced them.' He concluded, 'As far as this sceptic and cynicist is concerned, graphology is now serious and legitimate.'

Good letter formation, clear separation of lines, clear 'i' dots and paragraphs: good memory.

Regularity and angle: resistance to authority.

Wide spacing between letters, but space between 'm' and 'n' upward stroke narrow; narrow margins: defensiveness.

Arcades: deeper feelings hidden.

Intelligence and personality

The personality level of this writer is somewhat above average and he is fairly bright.

His handwriting shows a logical train of thought and sufficient critical judgement. Within the area of his knowledge he is usually capable of establishing an effective order of priorities and can usually penetrate to the essentials.

He has a good retentive memory and can apply knowledge and experience in practical situations. His way of thinking is not imaginative and he is not entirely free from traditional restraints. He is reluctant to deviate from an accepted method and not always receptive to new ideas. However, his handwriting shows a practical intellect and common sense.

Attitude towards work

This writer is an ambitious man who proceeds with steady energy in the accomplishment of his tasks. He is persistent and tenacious. He has the motivation to succeed and won't give up without a fight. He tackles his work with vigour and drive and will not easily be deflected from the course he has set. He has the determination to get things done. The writer can cope with pressure and enjoys achieving goals in the face of obstacles. He likes to work independently and relies mainly on his own abilities. He is inclined to go about things his own way and resists authority.

In his work he is thorough and he has the ability to double check. He pays attention to detail. He can concentrate on his work, do one thing at a time and ignore intrusions.

The handwriting shows a practical, logical and prudent person, who does not like to take risks. He does not make up his mind hastily on matters of importance, but is likely to weigh the pros and cons before deciding.

The writer is no pioneer and his problem-solving is not innovative, but he is a practical, down-to-earth man and in handling familiar tasks he can be relied upon to act sensibly and incisively.

Attitude towards others

This writer is usually well-mannered and polite in his behaviour towards others. He is presentable and capable of making a good impression.

He is able to impose his will and inspire confidence in others. His instructions are usually clear and easy to follow. He can pass on knowledge and experience to others. However, his handwriting also shows a lack of flexibility, indicating that his personality characteristics are based on defensiveness. He usually seems a bold, outspoken and self-confident person, but his handwriting shows an over-compensated insecurity. The result of this is a constant need to prove himself, which leads to some relentlessness. It is difficult for him to cope with objection or the questioning of his authority, whereby he may become somewhat rigid.

In his opinions he tends to be rather dogmatic, which sometimes leads to a lack of tolerance. He is self-assertive and wants his own way. This may cause situations to arise when he is somewhat arrogant. Once he has made up his mind he is seldom willing to compromise. However, he can exercise self-control when he needs to and can usually find the right tone.

On the surface this writer appears to others to be outgoing, but he keeps his deeper feelings out of reach. He is fairly tight-lipped and quite good at hiding his motives from other people. He has a prudent, careful and somewhat reticent nature. Reason controls his emotions.

Report No.3

Male 62, Management Consultant would like to know your analysis of his handwriting. Should he have done what a psychological report suggested 40 years ago: journalism or textile & colour design? The fact is that I actually like what I do and whatever I did, otherwise

Angle and regularity: strength of will that rarely permits compromise; will-power dominant, feelings play a secondary part.

Pastosity: sense of colour; warmth of feeling.

Regularity: self-control; dislike of spontaneous expression.

Terminal arcade: caution; calculation; mistrust.

Pastosity and regularity and terminal arcades: basic warmth of feeling and generosity, curbed by self-control as a result of scepticism.

Hooks in lower zones: need to hang onto material possessions.

Intelligence and personality

This writer's personality level is above average and his handwriting indicates a good intelligence.

His intellect is sharply observing and clarifying. He can make logical deductions. His handwriting shows a well-developed 'helicopter' view – he can penetrate to the essentials and is capable of establishing an effective order of priorities. He is also able to co-ordinate various factors quickly and to place them in a wider context.

He has a good retentive memory and can easily apply his knowledge and skills in practical situations.

Attitude towards work

This man is a go-getter, full of vitality. His handwriting shows great determination and energy. He is very strong-willed and often doggedly persistent.

His handwriting shows hard drive and goal-mindedness. He will almost never be deflected from the course he has set and he is aggressive in tackling problems. He enjoys achieving goals in the face of obstacles.

This writer is not afraid of making decisions and assuming responsibility for getting things done. He is inclined to go about things his own way. He does not follow the dictates of others, relying mainly on his own abilities.

His handwriting shows sound commercial skills. He has business ability and market awareness. He can spot new developments, is quick to see opportunities and has the ability to achieve targets.

This is a well-organized man, thorough, methodical and factual. He does not make up his mind hastily on matters of importance and, although decisive, he usually shows considerate care and restraint in his actions and decision-making. If necessary, he is willing to take calculated risks, but he is never impulsive.

Attitude towards others

The handwriting shows that this man presents himself skilfully and understands the importance of creating a good image. He is usually polite and well-mannered. He is able to maintain contact at all levels. He is a good negotiator, usually coming over to others as a person with authority and presence.

He is an excellent man-manager and a bold and self-confident person. He is able to impose his will to inspire confidence in others.

However, he is not as easy-going as he may seem at first

sight. He has decided and fixed opinions and once he has made up his mind he will be determined to get his own way. He has a somewhat relentless, inflexible side to him and his tenacity and will-power sometimes lead to a lack of tolerance. He pretends to listen to others, but is not really inclined to take advice and usually does exactly what he wants.

The handwriting shows some aggressiveness which has been over-compensated, resulting in the need to act, the need to achieve. He channels his aggressiveness into hard drive and goal-mindedness. He has great strength of will, but it is a strength of will that rarely permits compromise. He has a good outward bearing, often is polite, even charming in his behaviour towards others, but he won't take no for an answer.

He may also get impatient with people who are less quick on the uptake than he is himself and, if unable to implement his ideas, at times he reacts strongly. However, he generally exercises good self-control and is able to find the right tone in his behaviour towards others.

Although this man appears on the surface to be outgoing, he keeps his deeper feelings out of reach. He is quite good at hiding his motives from others. Will-power is the dominant feature of this writer's character. Feelings have been suppressed for so long that they play a secondary part in his life. On issues that really matter to him personally he will not give himself away. He relates to others pleasantly, but more or less superficially. His handwriting indicates a dislike of close involvement.

The writer usually makes a relaxed and outgoing impression, but in reality exercises a severe self-control.

Useful addresses

Belgium

La Société Belge de Graphologie
Avenue de Broqueville 227
1200 Brussels

Canada

Association des Graphologues
1340 Est Sainte Catherine
CP 215 Succ. C.
Montreal, Quebec H2L 4K1

Saskatchewan Handwriting Analysis Club
709 Main Street
Saskatoon
Saskatchewan S7H 0J9

France

Fédération Nationale des
Graphologues Professionnels
2 bis rue Roger Simon Barboux
94110 Arcueil

Société de Graphologie d'Aquitaine
9 place du Parliament
33000 Bordeaux

Germany

Internationale Gesellschaft für
Dynamische und Klinische
Schriftpsychologie (DKS)
Erlenweg 14
D–7000 Stuttgart 70

Israel

Naftali Institute for Handwriting
Analysis
52 Brodezki Street
Ramat Aviv

Italy

Istituto Grafologico G. Moretti
Piazza San Francesco 7
61029 Urbino (ps)

The Netherlands

ABG
International Association for Business
Graphology
PO Box 3850
1001 AR Amsterdam

Spain

Asociacion Grafopsicologica
Pez, 27—Primero Dcha
28004 Madrid

Sociedad Espanola de Grafologia
Apartado 40099
28007 Madrid

Sweden

Svenska Skriftpsykologiska
Foreningen
Muraragatan 14a
S–652 28 Karlstad

United Kingdom

The Academy of Graphology
1 Queen's Elm Square
London SW3 6ED
Training, exams.

The British Institute of
  Graphologists
4th floor
Bell Court House
11 Blomfield Street
London EC2M 7AY
Lectures, training, exams.

John A. Beck
The Graphology Society
33 Bonningtons
Thriftwood
Hutton
Brentwood
Essex
CM13 2TL
*Lectures on graphology and Jungian
psychology.*

Mrs A. Cooksey
BIG Bookshop
Bishops Close
Sonning
Reading
RG4 0ST
*Sells a wide variety of books on
graphology.*

Graph-O-Logica Ltd
48 Oakleigh Park South
London N20 9JN
*Occupational handwriting analysis, fraud
detection, questioned documents.*

United States of America

American Association of Handwriting
  Analysts
35970 Perth
Livonia, Michigan 48154

American Handwriting Analysis
  Foundation
PO Box 6201
San José, California 95150

American Society for Professional
  Graphologists
9109 North Branch Drive
Bethesda, Maryland 20817

Handwriting Analysts International
1504 West 29th Street
Davonport, Iowa 52804

The Institute of Graphological
  Science
3685 Ingleside Drive
Dallas, Texas 75229

National Society for Graphology
250 W. 57th Street, Suite 2032
New York, New York 10107

Bibliography

Handwriting analysis

Amend, Karen and Ruiz, Mary S., *Handwriting Analysis: The Complete Basic Book* (Newcastle Publishing Co. Inc., North Hollywood, California, USA, 1980).
_____ *Achieving Compatibility with Handwriting Analysis. Vol. 1: Exploring your Emotional Relationships; Vol. 2: Understanding your Sexual Relationships* (Newcastle Publishing Co. Inc., North Hollywood, California, USA, 1992).
Beauchataud, Gabrielle, *Learn Graphology – A Practical Course in 15 Lessons* (Scriptor Books, Quinta Drive, Barnet, Hertfordshire, UK, 1988).
Bernard, Marie, *The Art of Graphology* (The Whitston Publishing Co., Troy, New York, USA, 1985).
Branston, Barry, *Graphology Explained* (Piatkus Books, 1989).
Greene, James and Lewis, David, *The Hidden Language of your Handwriting* (Pan Books, 1982).
Gullan-Whur, Margaret, *Discover Graphology* (The Aquarian Press, 1991).
Hartford, Huntingdon, *You Are What You Write* (Peter Owen Ltd., Holland Park Avenue, London W11, UK, 1975).
Hearns, Rudolph S., *Handwriting, An Analysis through its Symbolism* (American Association of Handwriting Analysts, 1979).
Jacoby, H.J., *Analysis of Handwriting* (British Institute of Graphologists, 1991).
Koren, Anna, *The Secret Self – A Comprehensive Guide to Handwriting Analysis* (Adama Books, 1987).
Link, Betty, *Advanced Graphology* (Personnel Consultants and Publishers Inc., Chicago, Illinois, USA).
Mendel, Alfred O., *Personality in Handwriting* (Newcastle Publishing Co., Inc. North Hollywood, California 1980).
Nezos, Renna, *Graphology – The Interpretation of Handwriting* (Century Hutchinson, 1986).
Roman, Klara G., *Handwriting: A Key to Personality* (Pantheon Books, 1952).
Saudek, Robert, *The Psychology of Handwriting* (Books for Professionals, 1978).
_____ *Experiments with Handwriting* (Books for Professionals, 1978).

Simpson, Diane, *The Analysis of Handwriting, Personality and Character* (A & C Black, 1985).

Singer, Eric, *A Manual of Graphology* (Duckworth, 1987).

Whiting, Eldene Traitmatch, *Discovering the Occupational Personality Through Handwriting Analysis* (Padre Productions, Pismo Beach, California, 1989).

German

Müller, W. H. and Enskat, A., *Graphologische Diagnostik* (Verlag Hans Huber, Bern, Stuttgart, 1987)

Jobs and Careers

Careers Guide 1992/3 (CASCAID, Glenfield, Leicester, UK).

Occupations 1992 COIC (Careers and Occupational Information Centre, HMSO, Room E405, Moorfoot, Sheffield, S1 4PQ)

MANAGEMENT

Grey, Jerry L. and Starke, Frederick A., *Organizational Behaviour Concepts and Applications* (Merrill Publishing Co., Columbus, Ohio, USA, 1988).

The Human Resource Management Year Book (AP Information Services Ltd, 1992).

Psychology and testing

Appignanesi, Richard and Zarate, Oscar, *Freud for Beginners* (Icon Books, 1992).

Cohen, Ronald Jay et al, *Psychological Testing – An Introduction to Tests and Measurement* (Mayfield Publishing Co., 1240 Villa St., Mountain View, California, USA, 1988).

Jung, Carl J., *Man and his Symbols* (Penguin Books, 1964).

Kline, Paul, *Psychology Exposed or The Emperor's New Clothes* (Routledge, Chapman and Hall, 1988).

Roth, Ilana, ed., *The Open University's Introduction to Psychology, Volumes 1 and 2* (The Open University, Milton Keynes, UK, 1990).

General

de Bono, Edward, *I am right, you are wrong* (Penguin Books, 1991).

Evans, Peter and Deehan, Geoff, *The Keys to Creativity* (Grafton, 1990).

Eysenck, Hans and Michael, *Mind-Watching* (Prion, Gordon House Road, London NW5, UK, 1989).

Hilton, Ordway, *Scientific Examination of Questioned Documents* (Elsevier/Forensic and Police Science, 1984).

Moir, Anne and Jessel, David, *Brain Sex – The real difference between men and women* (Michael Joseph/Mandarin, 1991).

Index

Figures in **bold type** (**67**) refer to major discussions of the subject; those in *italic type* (*67*) refer to illustrations; and those in Roman type (67) direct you to minor references.